This tract is distributed free of charge in the interest of reaching every truth-seeking mind that desires to escape the path that leads to destruction of both body and soul.

TRACT NO. 3

Third Edition

The Universal Publishing Association

P.O. Box 24027

Waco, Texas 76702

UniversalPublishing.com

ISBN: 978-1-962573-20-7

Confused Because Essential

Though it is the crowning work of our salvation and of the setting up of the kingdom of Christ upon earth, yet the "investigative judgment" is one of the least understood and most mystified and confused Bible subjects of the age. Were it not essential to our salvation, the enemy would not have expended every possible effort to envelop it in darkness. Imperative, then, is the unremitting need to search the Scriptures "as for hidden treasure," and to beseech God for the guidance of His Spirit in order rightly to understand this all-important subject. In vain, though, *any* search for truth unless the motive be to learn and to do the will of God. Hence, "if any man," says Jesus, "will do His will, he shall know of the doctrine, whether it be of God." John 7:17.

Since the subject of the judgment is taught in types and in parables, and since the Lord explains that His teaching parabolically is so that only His disciples may know the mysteries of the kingdom of heaven (Matt. 13:11), obviously, therefore,

*None But His Followers Can Understand
the Whole Truth.*

"The kingdom of heaven," He says, "is like unto treasure hid in a field; the which when a man hath found, he hideth, and for joy thereof goeth and selleth all that he hath, and buyeth that field. Again, the kingdom of heaven is like unto a merchant man, seeking goodly pearls: who, when he had found one pearl of great price, went and sold all that he had, and bought it." Matt. 13:44-46.

In these parables, Christ clearly sets forth present truth as the indispensable condition to the establishing of His kingdom, and supreme effort as the indispensable condition to entering into it. Thus "none," declares the Spirit of Prophecy, "but those who have fortified the mind with the truths of the Bible will stand through the last great conflict. To every soul will come the searching test, Shall I obey God rather than men? The decisive hour is even now at hand. Are our feet planted on the rock of God's immutable Word?"—*The Great Controversy*, pp. 593, 594.

Let us come out of the stupor of presuming on God's grace, yet regarding Him responsible for any consequent issue of our life. He has perfectly done His part in fully charting the narrow path to the kingdom; now let us do our honest best to follow therein to the end of the way, for the joy that awaits us there! But never shall we do so save in returning to the old landmarks by forsaking the Devil, who has turned God's people from "the Way, the Truth, and the life" (John 14:6), into "a way which seemeth right unto a man," but the end of which "are the ways of death." Prov. 14:12.

The
Judgement and the Harvest in Testimony, Parable, Ceremony, and Number

In the Light of the Testimonies of the Prophets

Since by some the position is stoutly maintained that this all-important truth cannot be established by the Scriptures alone, let the reader therefore give attention to what the Bible says:

"I beheld *till* the thrones were *cast down*, and the Ancient of days did sit, Whose garment was white as snow, and the hair of His head like the pure wool: His throne was like the fiery flame, and His wheels as burning fire. A fiery stream issued and came forth from before Him: thousand thousands ministered unto Him, and ten thousand times ten thousand stood before Him: the *judgment was set, and the books were opened*." Dan. 7:9, 10.

In this scripture are set forth four pertinent facts: (1) the thrones were not present prior to the opening of the scene envisioned; (2) the Ancient of days came and did sit when the thrones were set up; (3) then the books were opened; (4) all of which (thrones, Ancient of days, and books) reveal a judgment scene. And since the books are obviously the focal point in the scene, the question naturally arises,

What Is the Reason for Books?

Fundamental to a correct concept of the judgment, is a correct understanding of the nature of it and of the reason for the books. As to the latter, John the Revelator says:

"And I saw the dead, small and great, stand before God; and the books were opened: and another book was opened, which is the Book of Life: and the dead were judged out of those things which were written in the books." Rev. 20:12.

Unquestionably, therefore, the books contain both the names and the records of all who are to be judged. And naturally these names and records were entered while each person was living. "Thine eyes," says the Psalmist, "did see my substance, yet being unperfect; and in Thy book all my members were written, which in continuance were fashioned, when as yet there was none of them." Ps. 139:16. "The Lord shall count, when He writeth up the people, that this man was born there." Ps. 87:6.

Thus does Inspiration reveal that each one's deeds are chronicled with terrible exactness in the books of heaven, and that in the reason for the books inheres the

That not every name that has been entered in the Lamb's books will be retained there, is born out with sad conclusiveness by the following scriptures:

"And the Lord said unto Moses, Whosoever hath sinned against Me, him will I blot out of My book." Ex. 32:33. "And if any man shall take away from the words of the book of this prophecy, God shall take away his part out of the Book of Life, and out of the holy city, and from the things which are written in this book." Rev. 22:19.

Accordingly, the books contain the names of a mixed multitude,—both those who stood firmly in the faith and continued patiently to the end, and those who did not. Said Christ: "He that shall endure unto the end, the same shall be saved." Matt. 24:13. But those who do not endure shall be lost.

"And these are they likewise which are sown on stony ground; who, when they have heard the Word, immediately receive it with gladness; and have no root in themselves, and so *endure but for a time*: afterward, when affliction or persecution ariseth for the Word's sake, immediately they are offended." Mark 4:16,17.

"O Lord, the hope of Israel, all that forsake Thee shall be ashamed, and they that depart from Me shall be written in the earth, because they have forsaken the Lord, the fountain of living waters." Jer. 17:13.

So, there must come a day of reckoning, a day when the names of those who are found unworthy of eternal life will be blotted out of the Lamb's Book of Life—a proceeding for which the only correct term can be, "investigative judgment."

And now that the "time is come that judgment must begin at the house of God. . . ," "thou therefore endure hardness, as a good soldier of Jesus Christ" (2 Tim. 2:3), for "if it [the judgment] first begin at us, what shall the end be of them that obey not the gospel of God?" 1 Pet. 4:17.

Since, therefore, in the fullness of time, the judgment will begin in the house of God, the church, each one is confronted with the imperative need to know

How Names Are Retained in the Book.

At the moment we accept Christ as our personal Saviour through the Word of Truth,—at that supreme moment God forgives us our sins, and the hands bloodstained by Calvary inscribe our names in the Lamb's Book of Life. Then simultaneously the pen of angels begins in the heavenly ledger the life or death chronicle of our Christian experience separate from our past. Even "the very hairs of your head are all *numbered.*" Matt. 10:30. Therefore "suffer not thy mouth to cause thy flesh to sin; neither say thou *before the angel*, that it was an error." Eccles. 5:6. For in the investigative judgment the books are opened and the deeds done in the flesh are brought to light for a final reckoning before the Ancient of days. All who have stood fast to the end will then forever have their sins blotted from the books and their names retained therein; while all who are not overcomers will then forever have their sins retained in the books and their names blotted therefrom.

Always man's greatest test, and one which has ever involved almost an instantaneous decision, has been in the unrolling of the scroll—in the eclipse of a past message by a new one,—present truth. On every such occasion each one has had to decide: Shall I heed the new and unpopular truth and walk in its light, joining with those who are despised by nearly every religious leader in the land? or shall I allow myself to be deterred by the decision and counsel of the ministry in my church?

When the judgment begins and the books open and the cases of each generation pass in succession in review before the judicial tribunal, some generations suffer an almost wholesale blotting out of names instead of sins. When the generation of Christ's first advent is weighed in the balance of the sanctuary, a whole nation will be found wanting and their names will be wiped from the book. And so in varying degree it has been at the introduction of every message in every age. "Different periods in the history of the church have each been marked by the development of some special truth, adapted to the necessities of God's people at that time. Every new truth *has made its way* against hatred and opposition; those who were blessed with its light were tempted and tried."—*The Great Controversy*, p. 609.

Accordingly, "when a message comes in the name of the Lord to His people, no one may excuse himself from an investigation of its claims."—*Testimonies on Sabbath-School Work*, p. 65. Lay aside all prejudices, self-opinions, and ideas of men who bear not the mark of Inspiration, and who say in effect by their actions: "I am rich, and increased with goods, and have need of nothing" (truth or prophets). Rev. 3:17.

The Bible can be rightly explained only by the Spirit Who dictated it. He "will guide you into all truth: for He shall not speak of Himself; but whatsoever He shall hear, that shall He speak: and He will shew you things to come" that ye may "be established in the present truth." And "whosoever . . . blasphemeth against the Holy Ghost [speaketh evil against the message] it shall not be forgiven" him: for it is the only means whereby we may be saved (John 16:13; 2 Pet. 1:12; Luke 12:10).

Consequently, the greatest danger of the people has not been their listening to error but rather their rejecting present truth. "If a message comes," saith the Lord, "that you do not understand, take pains that you may hear the reasons the messenger may give, . . . then produce your strong reasons; for your position will not be shaken by coming in contact with error."—*Testimonies on Sabbath-School Work*, pp. 65, 66. "Wherefore let him that thinketh he standeth take heed lest he fall." 1 Cor. 10:12.

Clearly, therefore, any attitude which disposes one not to make a candid investigation of any message that purports to be additional truth, must inevitably bring ruin upon oneself. While on the other hand he who accepts the truth but fails faithfully to live and to proclaim it, thereby brings upon himself ruin also— that against which Ezekiel warns: "When a righteous man doth turn from his righteousness, and commit iniquity, and I lay a stumblingblock [a message] before him, he shall die: because *thou hast not* given him warning, he shall die in his sin, and his righteousness which he hath done shall not be remembered; but his blood will I require *at thine hand*. Nevertheless if thou warn the righteous man, that the righteous sin not, and he doth not sin, he shall surely live, because he is warned; also thou *hast delivered thy soul.*" Ezek. 3:20, 21. But the wicked shall "be blotted out of the book of the living, and not be written with the righteous." Ps. 69:28.

Thus solidly established, the foregoing position on the investigative judgment makes all opposing positions

Unfounded Conclusions.

Because of their erroneous belief that God's throne has always been in the sanctuary and that Christ after ascending on high sat there at the right hand of His Father, men have put forth every effort possible to prove that Christ entered 'within the veil' immediately after He left His disciples. But as all such efforts, albeit ever so well-meaning in the interest of truth, are put forth by minds inspired, not by the Spirit of Truth, but rather by preconception, we must therefore diligently entreat the Lord for the promised Comforter to lead us into all truth, and to save us from being presumptuous and from blindly taking things for granted and forming conclusions without digging beneath the surface.

"We have also a more sure word of prophecy," says the apostle Peter; "whereunto ye do well that ye take heed, as unto a light that shineth in a dark place, until the day dawn, and the day star arise in your hearts: knowing this first, that no prophecy of the scripture is of any private interpretation. For the prophecy came not in old time by the will of man: but holy men of God spake as they were moved by the Holy Ghost." 2 Pet. 1:19-21.

The wise reader, therefore, will henceforth cease giving place to human theories and speculations which tempt him to the uttermost to make flesh his arm. He will instead attend diligently to Bible prophecy and to inspired interpretations, and will learn therefrom that the sanctuary is

God's Temporary Throne Room.

Since earthly beings, themselves having never been in heaven, are naturally strangers to heaven's realities (1 Cor. 2:9), then in order for God to make heavenly truth known unto them, He must reveal it by means of earthly realities with which they are familiar. Hence through the sanctuary work on earth is seen the sanctuary work in heaven (Heb. 9:1-9). Indeed, the sanctuary above being the pattern of the one below, the services of the former are therefore definitely revealed in the services of the latter. And the fact that the earthly sanctuary was appointed as a place for confession and for forgiveness of sins, shows that the throne-room in the heavenly sanctuary is only temporary. From it, while sin exists, the Lord carries on the work of removing from the universe sin and sinners. And this light in turn clearly shows that not until after sin came into the universe could the sanctuary congruously have existed in heaven.

"I looked," exclaimed the Revelator about 96 A. D., upon being shown the throne in the sanctuary, "and behold, a door was opened in heaven: and the first voice which I heard was as it were of a trumpet talking with me; which said, Come up hither, and I will shew thee things which must be hereafter.

"And immediately I was in the Spirit: and, behold, a throne was *set* in heaven, and One sat on the throne. And He that sat was to look upon like a jasper and a sardine stone: and there was a rainbow round about the throne, in sight like unto an emerald. And round about the throne were four and twenty seats: and upon the seats I saw four and twenty elders sitting, clothed in white raiment; and they had on their heads crowns of gold. And out of the throne proceeded lightnings and thunderings and voices: and there were seven lamps of fire burning before the throne, which are the seven Spirits of God. And before the throne there was a sea of glass like unto crystal: and in the midst of the throne, and round about the throne, were four beasts full of eyes before and behind."

"And I beheld, and, lo, in the midst of the throne and of the four beasts, and in the midst of the elders, stood a Lamb as it had been slain, having seven horns and seven eyes, which are the seven Spirits of God sent forth into all the earth. . . . And I beheld, and I heard the voice of many angels round about the throne and the beasts and the elders: and the number of them was ten thousand times ten thousand,

and thousands of thousands." Rev. 4:1-6; 5:6,11.

Here is brought to view a twofold scene. On the one hand, before the throne are the "seven lamps burning" and the "Lamb as it had been slain," showing that the throne was "set" there to serve in time of probation. The light from the candlestick represents the light of truth in the church while the blood of the Lamb is atoning for sinful beings. On the other hand, upon the throne sits the Ancient of days, the Judge, surrounded by the jury of twenty-four elders plus the angelic witnesses, "ten thousand times ten thousand, and thousands of thousands" of them, plus the four beasts (who, being "redeemed" "out of every kindred, and tongue, and people, and nation"—verses 8, 9,—are therefore symbolical of the saints,—all those whose sins will be blotted from the books of records,—just as the beasts of Daniel 7 are symbolical of all the kingdoms which will perish in their sins), with the Lamb, our Advocate, in the midst. All this shows a combined mediatorial-judicial work.

Now so far, we see that when John in vision beheld the door—the veil—as it opened to the Most Holy apartment of the heavenly sanctuary, he was permitted to look within, and that the things which he saw, were to take place "hereafter" from his time; showing thereby that at the time of his vision (about 96 A. D.) the Most

—15—

Holy apartment was closed. In addition to this, we shall now see from Daniel's prophecy that the *judgment throne was set up* in the Most Holy apartment of the heavenly sanctuary *after the "little horn"* of Daniel 7 *came up*.

"I considered the horns," says the seer, "and, behold, there came up among them another little horn, before whom there were three of the first horns plucked up by the roots: and, behold, in this horn were eyes like the eyes of man, and a mouth speaking great things. I beheld till the thrones were cast down, and the Ancient of days did sit, Whose garment was white as snow, and the hair of His head like the pure wool: His throne was like the fiery flame, and His wheels as burning fire. A fiery stream issued and came forth from before Him: thousand thousands ministered unto Him, and ten thousand times ten thousand stood before Him: the judgment was set, and the books were opened." Dan. 7:8-10.

These verses reveal that after "the judgment was set, and the books were opened," "the Son of man," Christ, was then "brought" to a position, not at "the right hand of God," "the Ancient of days," but "near *before*" Him (Dan. 7:8-10, 13).

Both John's and Daniel's visions reveal that the throne in the sanctuary was not there from the beginning of the creation of God; or from the days of Moses; or yet from the hour that Christ ascended on high; or even from the days of pagan Rome; that, indeed, it was not "set up" until after the fall of pagan Rome, when the "little horn" of the *non-descript* beast came up—in the days of Ecclesiastical Rome (Dan. 7:7-12, 21, 22). Elsewhere than in the sanctuary, therefore, is

God's Eternal Throne Room.

Because the sanctuary throne was not in existence in the days of the early Christian church, therefore the throne upon which Stephen saw Christ at the 'right hand of God' (Acts 7:56) could not have been in the sanctuary, wherein is the "sea of glass," but rather in Paradise, whence flows the "river of water of life," and on either side of which is "the tree of life." Rev. 22:1, 2. Very obviously, therefore, the throne which Stephen saw is "the throne of God and of the Lamb," the throne permanent and eternal. Round about *this* glory-seat are no beasts, no witnesses, no jury, and before it is "no candle," and no blood to be offered. In short, it stands, not in the sin-laden sanctuary, but in Paradise. It is the sovereign administrative throne, from which the Infinite eternally governs His immortal sinless beings!

To this throne, then, which is from everlasting to everlasting, Christ ascended and thereat sat down at the right hand of His Father until the time came when, in fulfilment of Daniel's prophecy and of John's revelation, sometime after the little-horn power came into existence, both He and His Father moved to the sanctuary throne. Upon the latter He does not *sit* as a king *at the right hand of God;* but rather *before* it does He stand both as a sacrificial lamb (Rev. 5:6), and as an intercessor (Dan. 7:13) pleading for sinful human beings. Hence, His mediatorial work began

First in the Holy, Then in the Most Holy.

In the earthly sanctuary the high priest (typifying Christ) officiated first in the holy apartment throughout the year, then upon the day of Atonement, the day of cleansing the sanctuary and judging the people, he officiated in the Most Holy for one day only. This twofold service signifies that in the heavenly sanctuary, the High priest, Christ, must necessarily first officiate in the holy apartment up to the antitypical day of Atonement, then during that day, He must officiate in the Most Holy apartment, before the throne. Thus the earthly services, too, repudiate the idea that Christ entered the Most Holy apartment of the heavenly sanctuary immediately after His ascension.

Very plainly, then, the ceremonial system reveals that from the time Christ "sat on the right hand of God" (Mark 16:19), where the "river of water of life" is, to the time that He and the Father moved to the throne in the sanctuary, where "the sea of glass" is (Dan. 7:9, 10; Rev. 4:6), He officiated in our behalf as a high priest in "the holy place" (Heb. 9:12); and that at the same time, conjointly with the Father, on the eternal sovereign throne ("the throne of God and of the Lamb"), He ruled the sinless universe.

From the foregoing facts, clear and dis-tinct, the only tenable conclusion to be drawn is that Christ, immediately after His ascension, rather that entering within the veil in the sanctuary, sat down at the right hand of His Father, in Paradise, and from there carried on His work in the holy apartment of the sanctuary.

How clear, already, the light of truth at last shining forth on this all important subject of salvation so long shrouded in the dense fog of human theories and speculations! And how solid the resultant vindication of the Spirit of Prophecy's reaffirmation of its position on the subject: "that the sanctuary question stands in righteousness and truth, just as we have held it for so many years."—*Gospel Workers*, p. 303.

"Cast not away therefore your confidence, which hath great recompense of reward. For ye have need of patience, that, after ye have done the will of God, ye might receive the promise. For yet a little while, and He that shall come will come, and will not tarry." Heb. 10:35-37.

"Now of the things which we have spoken this is the sum: We have such an high priest, Who is set on the right hand of the throne of the Majesty in the heavens; a minister of the sanctuary, and of the true tabernacle, which the Lord pitched, and not man." Heb. 8:1, 2.

"For Christ is not entered into the holy places made with hands, which are the figures of the true; but into heaven itself, now to appear in the presence of God for us." Heb. 9:24. Indeed, "now *once* in the end of the world hath He appeared to put away sin by the sacrifice of Himself. And as it is appointed unto men once to die, but after this the judgment" (Heb. 9:26, 27) —the cleansing of the sanctuary (Dan. 8:14).

Plainly, therefore, the judgment is to begin and the sanctuary to be cleansed, not before, but after, the fulfilment of the period for those appointed to die. The judging being consistent with the records found in the books of heaven, the names, therefore, of those who are found unworthy, without the "wedding garment" on, are blotted from the books. Thus is the sanctuary cleansed. Speaking of the commencement of this work of judging and cleansing, the angel said unto Daniel: "Unto two thousand and three hundred days; then shall the sanctuary be cleansed." Dan. 8:14.

Since the cleansing, accordingly, takes place at the termination of the 2,300 days, and since it is, as we have seen, the judgment, which takes place "in the end of the world" (Heb. 9:26), consequently the termination of the days, and the beginning of the mediatorial-judicial work of Christ are, upon the authority of Inspiration Itself, timed to the end of the world. Hence, conclusively, the 2,300 days do not end in the days of Antiochus Epiphanes, as some teach they do. This untenable position on the subject, along with other similarly unsupportable views on it, therefore makes necessary, in order to establish the very date of the cleansing, our first

Dispelling the Confusion Concerning the 2,300 days.

Those who are in opposition to the doctrine that the 2,300 days find their terminus in the end of the world, are, among themselves, at strong variance over when the days do, supposedly, end, just as they are over the truth of a multitude of other doctrines. Fully evident therefore is the fact that none of them have the truth on the subject. And yet in spite of this fact, they fail to see that the spirit which has led them into their present state of schism, doctrinal difference, strife, and confusion, unparalleled in history, cannot possibly be the Spirit of Truth, Who alone can lead them into the truth of the 2,300-day prophecy. Thus they continue darkening Christendom with what they imagine and proclaim to be light on it.

In the effort to support their position,

they bring in the Septuagint, the Vulgate, and the English Revised Version. These in the order named variously render the number in Daniel 8:14 as 2,400, 2,200, and 2,300 "evening morning." This difference alone is ample proof that the renderings are not the sound results of exact, literal translation of the verse; but rather are the product of interpretative translations of it, engendered of theological preconceptions on the subject.

Nevertheless, even these renderings as they stand, lend such feeble plausibility to the theories held in opposition to the doctrine that the 2,300 days terminate in the end of the world, as to compel the theorizers to read into Daniel 8:14 the word "sacrifice" so as to transform the "evening morning" phase of the text to read "evening morning sacrifices." Next, on the grounds that there were two sacrifices a day, they split the number of them in half. And the number being 2,400, 2,200, or 2,300, depending on which version they use, they get respectively 1,200, 1,100, 1,500 days! This adding-to and cutting-down, they then boldly put forth in proof of their theory! although there is no escaping the crystal-clear meaning of "evening morning" when viewed in the light of Genesis 1:5 which, as every Bible student well knows, can only mean a twenty-four hour period (both the night and the day), and which has nothing to do with sacrifices.

Very plainly, therefore, the numbers 2,400 and 2,200 and the interpolation of the word "sacrifices," are the vain results of false interpretation of Daniel's prophecies. The discrepancy between the two figures is due to the difference in the dates necessary to work out the different ideas on the text. Exposing both the ambition and the fate of those responsible for this vain attempt to place the fulfilment of the prophecy, the Lord declared unto Daniel: "Also the robbers of thy people shall exalt themselves to establish the vision; but they shall fall." Dan. 11:14.

Though the endeavor of these robbers of God's people to make the vision fit their ideas is doomed to failure, yet in their blind self-confidence they still try their best to establish it, even going so far in the effort as to make the writings of Josephus seem to speak as sacred history in support of their theory.

"And indeed it so came to pass," says the Jewish historian, in a passage which they most commonly use, "that our nation suffered these things under Antiochus Epiphanes, according to Daniel's vision and what he wrote years before they came to pass"—*Antiquities*, Book 12, Chapter 5.

Though Josephus does not even remotely allude to the number of days mentioned in Daniel 8:14, yet because he does apply the vision to the work of Antiochus Epiphanes, they in effect take him as a prophet inspired to interpret the Scriptures! Being merely a historian, though, and not a prophet, he accordingly, in writing the history of the Jews, made only a historical application of the similarity which he saw between Daniel's prediction and Antiochus' work. And such was well within his province as a historian. But his not having the gift of prophecy forbids God's people from accepting his applications of the Scriptures as authoritative and dependable.

From this sort of wresting, juggling, rationalizing, and explaining away of simple facts, the candid reader will see to what lengths men are going in order to dodge revealed truths which they do not like, and to lock arms with private theories to their liking. True indeed is the saying, "give a man a theory and the facts will come trooping after!"

With the mists of error now dispelled, our way is clear to proceed in ascertaining

When the 2,300 Days Begin and End.

From Daniel 7 it was seen that the throne of judgment or of cleansing was not to be set up until sometime after the little-horn power came into existence, while from Heb. 9:24-27 it was seen to be set up sometime before "the end of the world." Now to throw into full focus the light on the facts already brought forth, we must go to Daniel 8 and 11, to the express prophecy of the subject—the 2300 days.

Dan. 8:11, 12	Dan. 11:31
"Yea, he magnified himself even to the Prince of the host, and by him the daily sacrifice was taken away, and the place of His sanctuary was cast down. And an host was given him against the daily sacrifice by reason of transgression, and it cast down the truth to the ground; and it practised, and prospered."	"And arms shall stand on his part, and they shall pollute the sanctuary of strength, and shall take away the daily sacrifice, and they shall place the abomination that maketh desolate."

From this juxtaposition of Daniel 8:11, 12 and Daniel 11:31, the reader will observe that both scriptures are speaking of the same power. And Christ, predicting the signs of the end of the world, as He looked forward along the stream of time, declared: "When ye [His followers who were to be living at the time that this horn-power was at work against God, His truth, and His people] therefore shall see the abomination of desolation, spoken of by Daniel the prophet, stand in the holy place, (whoso readeth, let him understand:) then let them which be in Judaea flee into the mountains." Matt. 24:15, 16. These clear words of Christ Himself, place the work of this power in the future from His time.

Here Christ plainly states that at His time the abomination of desolation had not yet stood up "in the holy place," but that sometime in the Christian dispensation it would be seen to stand there. Still further, the angel instructed Daniel that at the time of the end shall be the vision (Dan. 8:13, 17). These two facts carry sweeping proof that the 2300-day period could not terminate until, following Christ's time, the daily be cast out and the abomination set up: for both of these events were to take place within the 2300 days.

This desolating power was, according to Daniel, to pollute by transgression the earthly sanctuary, or church. This was to be accomplished by casting down the Truth to the ground, by taking away the daily, and by bringing into the holy place "the abomination that maketh desolate," all of which was to be, said the angel, "unto two thousand and three hundred days;" and "then shall the sanctuary be cleansed."

From the weighty evidences here amassed, there is manifestly but one conclusion possible: the polluting of the holy place, the terminating of the 2300 days, and the cleansing of the sanctuary could not have taken place before Christ's time.

Facing the resounding finality of this threefold conclusion, the numerous voices which insistently localize within the Old Testament period the events bound up with the 2300 days, ought now to silence themselves completely and forever. But if they do not, then God, only, knows what they may next proclaim!

You cannot afford, brethren, now that the light is come, to let slip from you the opportunity of breaking away from the theories of men herein discredited by the "Spirit of Truth," and of placing your feet firmly on the solid foundation here established in their place by the testimony of Jesus Christ.

Upon this solid rock the structure of truth now in building will, as the reader can already see, withstand the most severe storm of both "wind" and "rain." So let us, in proceeding to erect its superstructure, liberally utilize, without the slightest fear of the coming storm (which will demolish and sweep away everything standing on a sandy foundation), the material so freely given:

To cleanse the earthly sanctuary, the abomination which the wicked power here under discussion, brought in, must necessarily be cast out, and then "the truth," also "the daily," which the same power trod down and cast out, must be restored. Very obviously, therefore, there is not the slightest room for doubt as to either the way in which the sanctuary was polluted or the way in which it must be cleansed.

The eighth chapter of the book of Daniel contains a vivid prophetic symbolism of two beasts (a ram and a he goat), concerning which the angel explained: "The ram which thou sawest having two horns are the kings of Media and Persia. And the rough goat is the king of Grecia." Dan. 8:20, 21.

". . . the he goat waxed very great: and when he was strong, the great horn was broken; and for it came up four notable ones toward the four winds of heaven. And out of one of them came forth a little horn, which waxed exceeding great, toward the south, and toward the east, and toward the pleasant land." Dan. 8:8, 9. ". . . the great horn that is between his eyes," explained the angel, "is the first king"—Alexander. "Now that being broken, whereas four stood up for it, four kingdoms shall stand up out of the nation, but not in his power"—not in Alexander's power; that is, not "to his posterity." Dan. 8:21, 22; 11:4.

"And in the latter time of their kingdom, when the transgressors [the Jews] are come to the full, a king of fierce countenance, and understanding dark sentences, shall stand up. And his power shall be mighty, but not by his own power [for "arms shall stand on his part" (Dan. 11:31)—the armies of the civil powers]: and he shall destroy wonderfully, and shall prosper, and practise, and shall destroy the mighty and the holy people." Dan. 8:23, 24.

Obviously, then, Daniel 8:22-24 is parallel with Daniel 7:25: "And he shall speak great words against the Most High, and shall wear out the saints of the Most High, and think to change times and laws: and they shall be given into his hand until a time and times and the dividing of time."

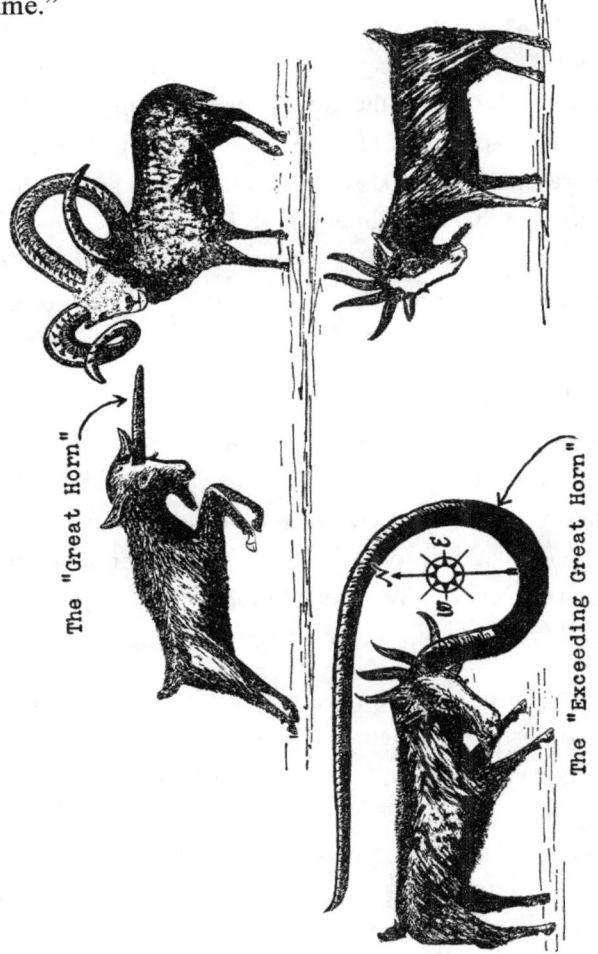

The "Great Horn"

The "Exceeding Great Horn"

Daniel had the vision in Babylon, northeast of "the pleasant land"—Palestine. From Babylon the exceeding great horn went first "south," next "east," then north in order to make the turn westward—"toward the pleasant land." Thus it went in all four directions, denoting that it became a world power. Moreover, also the "brass" of the great image of Daniel 2, which Daniel explains is to "bear rule over all the earth," represents Grecia. However, as neither the goat's first horn nor his subsequent four horns bore universal rule, then to fulfil the prophecy of the brass kingdom, his exceeding great horn must be the one to "bear rule over all the earth." Dan. 2:39.

Though the fourth beast of Daniel 7 shows that this desolating power is descended from Rome, the symbolism of the he goat goes further back to show that this world power originally descended from one of the Grecian divisions (Dan. 11:5), and later put on the garb of Christianity—the religion of "a god whom his fathers knew not." Verse 38.

Gradually assuming the ornaments of the sanctuary, he before long magnified himself against the Prince (Christ) of the host (the Christians). And disregarding "the god of his fathers," he ostensibly became Christianized, but at what cost to Christianity!—Not only was the "daily" "taken away," but also "the place of His sanctuary was cast down." In other words, he "cast down" the Lord's "place" and there set up his own—elevated himself to Christ's place.

The word "sacrifice" being supplied in connection with the word "daily," it manifestly does not belong to the text. Since, however, the English language does not have an exact equivalent of the Hebrew word "daily," which is variously rendered "continual," "perpetual," "everlasting," and since none of these terms are synonymous, but carry individual connotations, it is consequently imperative to take them all together as a compound word, so as to arrive at the exact truth. In view, therefore, of this fact, also the fact that the Sabbath doctrine is the only Bible doctrine in the Christian era that can possibly be designated as "daily" (pertaining to worship in respect to a day), as well as "continual," "perpetual," and "everlasting,"—from time immemorial to time eternal,—it is hence evident that all these various renderings can apply to no other doctrine than the Sabbath—the eternal rest day. And in divine certification of its perpetuity, ring on through the centuries from Sinai the immutable words:

"Wherefore the children of Israel shall keep the Sabbath, to observe the Sabbath throughout their generations, for a perpetual covenant. It is a sign between Me and the children of Israel for ever: for in six days the Lord made heaven and earth, and on the seventh day He rested, and was refreshed." Ex. 31:16, 17.

The horn's taking away the "daily," was therefore nothing other than his taking away from the Christian church the Lord's Sabbath and putting in its place Sunday worship, a pagan sabbath,—"abomination that maketh desolate,"—a desecration which grieved away God's presence from the church.

The ram and the he goat were shown to Daniel in vision "in the third year of the reign of king Belshazzar." Dan. 8:1. Daniel was "astonished at the vision, but none understood it." Verse 27. The time, moreover, had elapsed, and Jerusalem was still a waste. So later "in the first year of Darius," who "was made king over the realm of the Chaldeans" (Dan. 9:1), Daniel was shown "by books the number of the years, whereof the word of the Lord came to Jeremiah the prophet, that he would accomplish seventy years in the desolations of Jerusalem." Verse 2. Jerusalem, however, was still a desolation, though the time of the people's captivity according to prophecy was fulfilled, and the vision was still "none [not] understood," as is clearly seen from Daniel's prayer:

". . . I set my face unto the Lord God, to seek by prayer and supplications, with fasting, and sackcloth, and ashes: and I prayed unto the Lord my God. . . . O Lord, according to all Thy righteousness, I beseech Thee, let Thine anger and Thy fury be turned away from Thy city Jerusalem, Thy holy mountain: because for our sins, and for the iniquities of our fathers, Jerusalem and Thy people are become a reproach to all that are about us. Now therefore, O our God, hear the prayer of Thy servant, and his supplications, and cause Thy face to shine upon Thy sanctuary that is desolate, for the Lord's sake. . . .

"Yea, whiles I was speaking in prayer, even the man Gabriel, whom I had seen in the vision at the beginning [in the eighth chapter], being caused to fly swiftly, touched me about the time of the evening oblation . . . and said, . . . Seventy weeks are determined upon thy people and upon thy holy city, to finish the transgression, and to make an end of sins, and to make reconciliation for iniquity, and to bring in everlasting righteousness, and to seal up the vision and prophecy, and to anoint the Most Holy.

"Know therefore and understand, that from the going forth of the commandment to restore and to build Jerusalem unto the Messiah the Prince shall be seven weeks, and threescore and two weeks: the street shall be built again and the wall, even in troublous times. And after three-score and two weeks shall Messiah be cut off, but not for Himself: and the people of the prince that shall come shall destroy the city and the sanctuary; and the end thereof shall be with a flood, and unto the end of the war desolations are determined. And He shall confirm the covenant with many for one week: and in the midst of the week he shall cause the sacrifice and the oblation to cease, and for the overspreading of abominations He shall make it desolate, even until the consummation, and that determined shall be poured upon the desolate." Dan. 9:3-27.

The angel apportioned the seventy weeks into three periods: "seven weeks, and threescore and two weeks," and "one week." And though in his words to Daniel, quoted above, he explained the time prophesied, yet Daniel still did not fully understand the vision. As he did certainly, however, understand the angel's interpretation of the "ram" and of the "goat" to be symbolical of "Persia" and "Grecia" respectively, the work of "the exceeding great horn" was therefore what he did not understand. And so it was that later "in those days," he was again "mourning;" this time, "three full weeks." Whereupon he says:

I saw "a certain man clothed in linen, whose loins were girded with fine gold of Uphaz. . . . Then said he unto me, . . . Now I am come to make thee understand what shall befall thy people in the latter days:for yet the vision is for many days." "For at the time of the end shall be the vision." Dan. 10:5, 12, 14; 8:17.

That chapters 11 and 1 2 contain the explanation of the vision promised by the angel in chapter 10, can be readily recognized not only from the continuity of the angel's speech but also from the fact that these chapters are the explanation of the vision in the eighth chapter. For the reader's convenience, we quote the last two verses of chapter 10, and a part of the angel's explanation recorded in chapter 11:

"Then said he, Knowest thou wherefore I come unto thee? and now will I return to fight with the prince of Persia: and when I am gone forth, lo, the prince of Grecia shall come. But I will shew thee that which is noted in the Scripture of Truth: and there is none that holdeth with me in these things, but Michael your Prince."

"Also I in the first year of Darius the Mede, even I, stood to confirm and to strengthen him. And now will I shew thee the truth. Behold, there shall stand up yet three kings in Persia; and the fourth shall be far richer than they all: and by his strength through his riches he shall stir up all against the realm of Grecia. And a mighty king shall stand up, that shall rule with great dominion, and do according to his will. And when he shall stand up, his kingdom shall be broken, and shall be divided toward the four winds of heaven; and not to his posterity, nor according to his dominion which he ruled:

for his kingdom shall be plucked up, even for others beside those." Dan. 10:20, 21; 11:1-4.

It is evident that in this chapter the angel is explaining in detail "the vision" which was shown to Daniel in the eighth chapter, and that Daniel 8:11, 12 is parallel in time with Daniel 11:31. A comparison of both scriptures, as found on page 25, makes clear that the eleventh chapter is an explanation in particular of the exceeding great horn of the eighth chapter.

Also it makes clear that the sanctuary spoken of in Daniel 8:11 cannot be any other than God's sanctuary: for on the one hand a heathen structure can never be of strength or on the other hand be polluted when it has never been clean. And, moreover, never does the Bible call it a sanctuary.

And, finally, the very fact that the sanctuary in Jerusalem was neither polluted nor cleansed in the manner described by the angel, but was left desolate and was ultimately destroyed (Dan. 9:26), puts the riveting evidence to the proof that neither the polluting nor the cleansing took place in the Old Testament era.

This solid conclusion is made doubly fast by virtue of Christ's statement (page 25), placing the work of the desolating power in the Christian dispensation.

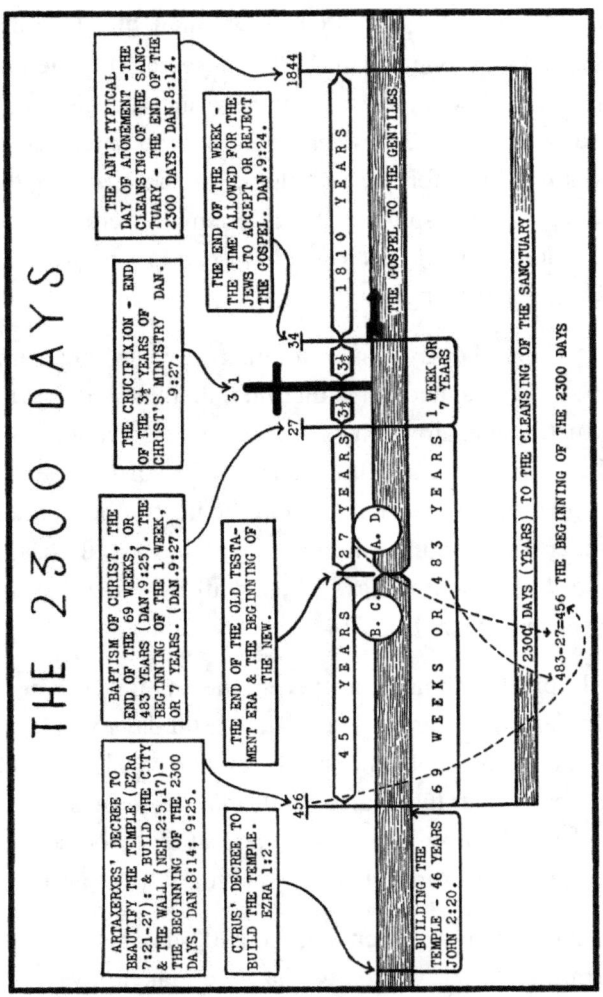

THE 2300 DAYS

ARTAXERXES' DECREE TO BEAUTIFY THE TEMPLE (EZRA 7:21-27) & BUILD THE CITY & THE WALL (NEH. 2:5,17)—THE BEGINNING OF THE 2300 DAYS. DAN. 8:14; 9:25.

CYRUS' DECREE TO BUILD THE TEMPLE. EZRA 1:2.

BUILDING THE TEMPLE - 46 YEARS. JOHN 2:20.

THE END OF THE OLD TESTAMENT ERA & THE BEGINNING OF THE NEW.

BAPTISM OF CHRIST, THE END OF THE 69 WEEKS, OR 483 YEARS (DAN. 9:25). THE BEGINNING OF THE 1 WEEK, OR 7 YEARS. (DAN. 9:27.)

THE CRUCIFIXION - END OF THE 3½ YEARS OF CHRIST'S MINISTRY DAN. 9:27.

THE END OF THE WEEK - THE TIME ALLOWED FOR THE JEWS TO ACCEPT OR REJECT THE GOSPEL. DAN. 9:24.

THE ANTI-TYPICAL DAY OF ATONEMENT - THE CLEANSING OF THE SANCTUARY - THE END OF THE 2300 DAYS. DAN. 8:14.

456 YEARS — 69 WEEKS OR 483 YEARS — 27 YEARS — 3½ — 3½ — 34 — 1810 YEARS

1 WEEK OR 7 YEARS

456 — 27 — 31 — 34 — 1844

THE GOSPEL TO THE GENTILES

2300 DAYS (YEARS) TO THE CLEANSING OF THE SANCTUARY

483-27=456 THE BEGINNING OF THE 2300 DAYS

There is no time other than the "two thousand and three hundred days" (Dan. 8:14) and the "seventy weeks" (Dan.

9:24), to which can apply the statement, "the time appointed was long." Dan. 10:1. But seeing that the former period was too long for restoring and cleansing the sanctuary in Jerusalem, and that the latter period was too long for the rebuilding of the city (for the seventy years spoken of by Jeremiah were already fulfilled), Daniel was prompted to cry out to the Lord for understanding.

"Then," he says, in continuing, "I heard one saint speaking, and another saint said unto that certain saint which spake, How long shall be the vision concerning the daily . . . , and the transgression of desolation, to give both the sanctuary and the host to be trodden under foot? And he said unto me, Unto two thousand and three hundred days; then shall the sanctuary be cleansed." Dan. 8:13, 14.

Expressed in modern speech, the angel's answer to Daniel's question would be that 2300 days would be required for "both the sanctuary and the host to be trodden under foot," also for the daily to be cast down and for the transgression of desolation to be set up, and that afterwards shall the sanctuary be cleansed.

In this light it is seen that the 2300-day period must terminate after "the daily" has been taken away and "the transgression of desolation" has been accomplished. Thus the taking away of "the daily" and the bringing in of "the abomination that maketh desolate" by the transgression of desolation, will "give both the sanctuary and the host to be trodden under foot."

The treading of the host is the massacring of the Christians who would not worship according to the dictates of the horn-power. The treading down of the sanctuary, the church, gave rise to the establishing of an earthly priesthood in the place of Christ, Who ministers from within the heavenly sanctuary.

And as the great horn of the he goat is symbolical of the Roman (iron—Dan. 2:40) world in its three periods,—pagan, ecclesiastical, and protestant,—also as in its second period, it trod the truth and the "host" under foot and polluted the sanctuary by bringing in the abominations while "it practised, and prospered" (Dan. 8:12), the 2300-day period, accordingly, extends beyond the fall of Ecclesiastical Rome and reaches into the Protestant period.

As furthermore, the commandment to rebuild Jerusalem went forth in 457 B.C. (Ezra 7:21- 27), the starting point of the seventy weeks proves to be one with that of the 2300 days.

And localizing Christ's ministry within this period, the angel said: ". . . He [Christ] shall confirm the covenant with many for one week: and in the midst of the week He shall cause the sacrifice and the oblation to cease." Dan. 9:27.

Since the confirming of the covenant with the many (the Jews) was accomplished during the seven years from the beginning of Christ's ministry, the time of His baptism, to the time Peter was commissioned to take the gospel to the Gentiles (Acts 10:28; read entire chapter), and since in the midst of this period Christ was crucified, "the week" proves to be seven literal years, and reveals that the 2300-day period must be computed by the rule of Ezekiel 4, reckoning a day for a year, thuswise:

". . . from the going forth of the commandment [found in Ezra 7:21-27] to restore and to build Jerusalem [the beginning of the 2300 days], unto the Messiah the Prince [to Christ at His baptism], shall be seven weeks [49 years], and threescore and two weeks [434 years]," totaling 483 years in all, with the first seven weeks, or forty-nine years, being for the rebuilding of the city.

Then after "seven weeks" plus "threescore and two weeks [483 years] shall Messiah be cut off, . . . and the people of the prince [the Romans] that shall come shall destroy the city and the sanctuary [fulfilled by Titus about 70 A. D.]; and the end thereof shall be with a flood, and unto the end of the war desolations are determined. And He [Christ] shall confirm the covenant with many for one week [seven years, beginning at His baptism]:

and in the midst of the week [in the midst of the seven years] He shall cause the sacrifice and the oblation to cease [by the sacrifice of Himself and by its transfer to the heavenly sanctuary: His sacrifice taking the place of the earthly sacrifice, and thus the heavenly sanctuary taking the place of the earthly sanctuary, with Christ Himself being the high priest], and for the overspreading of abominations He shall make it [the temple in Jerusalem] desolate [His presence completely removed], even until the consummation, and that determined shall be poured upon the desolate." Dan. 9:25-27.

The remainder of the 2300 days, or years, reach to the time of the cleansing of the sanctuary. (See illustration on page 37.)

Counting forward 2300 years from October 457 B.C., the terminus is October, 1844 A. D. And as the angel said, "Unto two thousand and three hundred days; *then* shall the sanctuary be cleansed," the cleansing must thence have commenced in 1844, the very year in which, for the first time in history, the first angel's message rang forth the proclamation: "Fear God, and give glory to Him; for the hour of His judgment is come" (Rev. 14:7; Dan. 7:9, 10)—the time that the Great Judge and the heavenly tribunal sit in judgment to separate the bad from the good; that is, to blot from the Book of Life the names of those who have entered the service of Christ but have not endured to the end.

Since this fearsome truth, as here revealed, finds its counterpart in Christ's parable of the wheat and the tares, the parables must necessarily therefore teach the investigative

Judgment Among the Living.

"Let both grow together," commands Christ, in regard to the commingling of the wheat and tares, "until the harvest: and in the time of harvest I will say to the reapers, Gather ye together first the tares, and bind them in bundles to burn them: but gather the wheat into My barn." Matt. 13:30.

Here the Lord is parabolically teaching that a time of investigation will come, and that then the angels will remove the sinners *from* "*the congregation of the righteous.*" Ps. 1:5.

"Again, the kingdom of heaven is like unto a net, that was cast into the sea, and gathered of every kind: which, when it was full, they drew to shore, and sat down, and gathered the good into vessels, but cast the bad away. So shall it be at the end of the world: the angels shall come forth, and sever the wicked from among the just." Matt. 13:47-49.

In both of these parables, Christ is sounding the forewarning that the investigative judgment will take place in the time called "harvest," which is the end of the world—the time in which the 2300 days culminate, just as the angel declared: "Understand, O son of man: for at the time of the end shall be the vision." Dan. 8:17. ". . . shut thou up the vision; for it shall be for many days." Dan. 8:26. ". . . for yet the vision is for many days." Dan. 10:14.

Pointing directly to the time that the investigative judgment shall take place among the living, Malachi parallels both parables in his prophecy:

". . . the Lord, Whom ye seek, shall suddenly come to His temple, . . . But who may abide the day of His coming? and who shall stand when He appeareth? for He is like a refiner's fire and like fuller's sope: and He shall sit as a refiner and purifier of silver: and He shall purify the sons of Levi, and purge them as gold and silver, that they may offer unto the Lord an offering in righteousness." Mal. 3:1-3.

As the cleansings called for in the parables and in Malachi's prophecy have never taken place, the investigative judgment of the living is obviously, then, yet future. This investigative work is therefore occasioned by the work of separation in the earthly sanctuary (church), as brought to view also in Ezekiel 9:

"And, behold, six men came from the way of the higher gate, which lieth toward the north, and every man a slaughter weapon in his hand; and one man among them was clothed with linen, with a writer's inkhorn by his side: and they went in, and stood beside the brasen altar. And the glory of the God of Israel was gone up from the cherub, whereupon he was, to the threshold of the house. And he called to the man clothed with linen, which had the writer's inkhorn by his side; and the Lord said unto him, Go through the midst of the city, through the midst of Jerusalem, and set a mark upon the fore-heads of the men that sigh and that cry for all the abominations that be done in the midst thereof.

"And to the others he said in mine hearing, Go ye after him through the city, and smite: let not your eye spare, neither have ye pity: slay utterly old and young, both maids, and little children, and women: but come not near any man upon whom is the mark; and begin at My sanctuary. Then they began at the ancient men which were before the house." Verses 2-6.

Here the people are shown to be in a mixed state (tares and wheat commingled), with the time just ahead of them when on the one hand those who have sighed and cried for the abominations in their midst shall receive the mark of deliverance, while on the other hand those who have not sighed and cried shall be left without the mark, to perish (in their sins) under the angels' slaughter weapons.

From this separation—the one in the church—come forth *the first fruits*.

Then follows the separation from among the nations, as seen in the parable of Matthew 25, prophetically describing Christ's coming, though not the one viewed in 1 Thessalonians 4:16, 17, for at the time of the latter, "the dead in Christ shall rise first: then we which are alive and remain shall be caught up together with them in the clouds, to meet the Lord in the air"; whereas at the time of the former, "when the Son of man shall come in His glory, and all the holy angels with Him, then shall He sit upon the throne of His glory [the kingdom-church, which up to this point consists only of the first fruits].

"And before Him shall be gathered all nations; and He shall separate them one from another, as a shepherd divideth his sheep from the goats: and He shall set the sheep on His right hand, but the goats on the left. Then shall the King say unto them on His right hand [these being the second fruits], Come, ye blessed of My Father, inherit the kingdom prepared for you from the foundation of the world. . . . Then shall He say also unto them on the left hand, Depart from Me, ye cursed, into everlasting fire, prepared for the devil and his angels." Matt. 25:31-34, 41.

From this separation—the one among the nations—come forth the second fruits.

The angels who are round about the throne in the heavenly sanctuary during the judgment of Daniel 7:9, 10 and of Revelation 5:11 shall, as the parables explain, descend with "the Son of man" when He comes "to His temple" (His church) to separate by judgment "the wicked from among the just," and to purge as gold and silver those "who may abide the day of His coming . . . that they may offer unto the Lord an offering in righteousness." Mal. 3:2, 3.

In graphic demonstration that He will come to earth with all His angels to execute judgment upon the living, the Lord revealed Himself prophetically to Ezekiel as being brought enthroned to earth by four living creatures just before the slaughter of the hypocrites in the church takes place. And as each of the living creatures has the face of a lion, the face of a calf, the face of a man, and the face of an eagle (Ezek. 1:10),—the same judicial insignia as have the beasts who are before the throne in the heavenly sanctuary (Rev. 4:7) in the time of the judgment of the dead,—and as they descend to earth, they thereby symbolically show that the work of the mediatorial-judicial throne which convenes and presides over the judgment of the dead is extended to earth.

This extension, so far as we are able to know now, must take place at the opening of the seventh seal (Rev. 8:1), for at that time the celestial voices, which opened the judgment of the dead, cease in the heavenly sanctuary and begin, after the half hour's silence, to sound on earth. In other words, just as in heaven at the opening of the judgment of the dead, there were "lightnings and thunderings and voices" (Rev. 4:5), likewise on earth at the opening of the "judgment of the living," there are "voices, and thunderings, and lightnings, and an earthquake." Rev. 8:5.

With the judgment of the dead, however, the work of separation takes place in the books in the heavenly sanctuary; whereas with the judgment of the living, the separation takes place among the people in the church as well as among their names in the books in the heavenly sanctuary, thus showing that both sanctuaries will finally be cleansed.

Inescapably, therefore, the Lord's coming to His temple (Mal. 3:1-3), His coming with all His angels (Matt. 25), and His coming enthroned above the living creatures (Ezek. 1),—all three representing the same event as has been shown,—take place at the beginning of the judgment of the living: the time in which the judicial activities of the heavenly sanctuary extend to the earthly sanctuary — the church.

"And I looked, and behold a white cloud," exclaimed John the Revelator, envisaging the same coming variously described by Malachi, Matthew, and Ezekiel, "and upon the cloud One sat like unto the Son of man, having on His head a golden crown, and in His hand a sharp sickle. And another angel came out of the temple, crying with a loud voice to Him that sat on the cloud, Thrust in Thy sickle, and reap: for the time is come for Thee to reap; for the harvest of the earth is ripe. And He that sat on the cloud thrust in His sickle on the earth; and the earth was reaped." Rev. 14:14-16.

This coming of the Son of man is plainly, therefore, not when the resurrected and the living righteous are caught up together to meet Him in the air: for verses 17-20, following the ones quoted in the paragraph above, reveal that after He came and reaped the earth, "another angel . . . having a sharp sickle" came and reaped a second harvest before the wrath of God—the seven last plagues (Rev. 15:1)—was poured out upon the wicked.

Thus again and for the fourth time it is seen that there are two different comings of the Son of man: the one to "sever the wicked from among the just" in the church (Matt. 13:49), and then immediately to call the just from among the wicked in

Babylon (Rev. 18:4); the other to take the saints, both the resurrected and the living, to the mansions which He has prepared for them (1 Thess. 4:16; John 14:1-3).

At the former coming of the Son of man, the stone which smote the great image was cut out without hands (without man's aid, and by the Lord Himself) because, as the Lord says, "there was none to help; and I wondered that there was none to uphold: therefore Mine own arm brought salvation unto Me; and My fury, it upheld Me. And I will tread down the people in Mine anger, and make them drunk in My fury, and I will bring down their strength to the earth." Isa. 63:5, 6.

This work of separation, or cleansing, brought to view in the parable of Matthew 13:30 and again in that of Matthew 13:47-49, also in the prophecy of Malachi 3:1-3 and in that of Ezekiel 9, as well as in Revelation 14, is directly applicable to the judgment day for the living; but the cleansing of the sanctuary at the end of the 2300 days, according to Daniel 8:14 and Daniel 7:9, 10, applies directly to the

Judgment Among the Dead.

Though the cleansing of the sanctuary, as has already been seen from Daniel's prophecies was to take place after 1844 A.D., yet since the living righteous are still commingled with the sinners in the church, and since Daniel saw the Ancient

—49—

of days sit in judgment, not to slay those who had "the mark," but to judge from "the books" which "were opened," obviously his vision of the judgment is in respect to the dead.

As to the cleansing of the church on earth, it is to be accomplished first by casting out the abomination, second by restoring the truth, and third by taking away the tares. But as to the cleansing of the sanctuary above, it is now being accomplished by removing from the Book of Life the names of those who are found wanting; then by placing them in the book which contains the names of those who are to come up in the resurrection of the wicked after the thousand years (Rev. 20:5); thereby leaving in the Book of Life the names only of those who have gained the victory over sin, and who thus are waiting to come up in the resurrection of the just (Rev. 20:6). John, accordingly, "saw the dead, small and great, stand before God; and the books were opened: and another book was opened, which is the Book of Life: and the dead were judged out of those things which were written in the books, according to their works." Verse 12.

Beyond the reasons already adduced, there are still

Further Reasons for Both Judgments.

As the cleansing of the heavenly sanctuary is a work of cleansing the books by blotting from them the names of both the backsliders and the tares, and as at the "time of trouble, such as never was since there was a nation," the only ones who "shall be delivered" are those whose names are found written in the book, the cleansing of the books, therefore, obviously takes place before the resurrection, and before the time of trouble such as never was. Thus the unfaithful dead will be left in their graves at the first resurrection, and the unfaithful living will be left without deliverance from the coming trouble. But were their names allowed to remain in the books, then according to the records either the wicked dead would have to be resurrected with the righteous, and the living wicked delivered with the living righteous or else both the righteous dead and the righteous living would have to be forsaken with them—alternatives both of which, of course, are impossible; thus again making mandatory an absolute separation, as instanced in type in Joshua's time:

"There is an accursed thing," said the Lord, "in the midst of thee, O Israel: thou canst not stand before thine enemies, until ye take away the accursed thing from among you. . . . And Joshua and all Israel with him, took Achan . . . and all that he had: . . . and all Israel stoned him." Josh. 7:13, 24, 25.

From this bulwark of evidence in proof of the cleansing of the church on earth and of the books in heaven, towers forth the impregnable truth that the living who, continuing faithful to the end, retain their names in the Book of Life, shall, in this time of separation, receive God's mark, or seal, of deliverance, while those who do not shall be left without it, to perish in their sins. And, correspondingly, the dead whose names are retained after the judgment, in the book of the dead, shall come forth in the first resurrection (Rev. 20:6), while those who were unfaithful in life wait until after the thousand years, to come forth with all the wicked in the second resurrection (verse 5).

So while it is necessary in the congregation of the dead to separate the wicked from the righteous now awaiting the resurrection morning, it is just as necessary in the congregation of the living to separate the wicked from the righteous now preparing for deliverance from the coming trouble, and awaiting the second coming of Christ—His visible coming to wake the dead saints and to take up both them and the living.

There are therefore two separations, one among the righteous dead and the other among the righteous living, the dead being appointed to resurrection and the living to translation.

Those, on the other hand, whose names shall be blotted out of the books are those who shall have failed to put on the "wedding garment." Matt. 22:11. At the Master's command (verse 13), they shall be cast out, never more to be among the wedding guests.

This cleansing of the Book of Life is further seen to be necessary in order to enable the angels rightly to select the saints, for when the Son of man comes with all His angels, He shall send them "with a great sound of a trumpet, and they shall gather together His elect [the resurrected] from the four winds, from one end of heaven to the other" (Matt. 24:31), and take them to join the living.

The concentrated light now shining forth from the prophecies herein viewed in their correlative connection, shows that both the sanctuary in heaven and the one on earth were polluted, not by the political and military conquests of heathen powers, but rather, first, by some of its converts' not enduring (Matt. 10:22); second, by Satan's bringing in the tares while men slept (Matt. 13:25); and third, by the exceeding great horn's casting out the "daily," treading down the truth, and bringing in the abomination that maketh desolate: thus involving both the earthly and the heavenly sanctuaries.

This startling revelation shows conclusively that the cleansing according to Daniel 8:14 is first of the sanctuary in heaven, and second of the sanctuary on earth.

Important as it is, any who would fail to make a diligent and careful study of the nature and significance of this great work of God's investigating the guests who have come in for the wedding, are simply indifferent to the prospects of eternal life—"so great salvation." For when a person's judgment is pending, and he is unaware of the fact, he will be unprepared and unable to stand when his case is investigated. To this all-important subject "therefore we ought to give the more earnest heed." Heb. 2:1. And in doing this, we must approach the judgment

In The Light of The Parables.

The seed-sower, the seed, the field, the season of cultivation and growing, and the season of harvest must together be perfectly calculated to illustrate the spiritual kingdom; otherwise the representation can only lead into error instead of into truth.

The four seasons of the year all being required in completing the process of planting, raising, and harvesting the year's crops, and Autumn being the beginning of the agricultural year (just as the close of the summer season is "the feast of *ingathering*, which is in the *end of the year*, when thou hast gathered in thy labours out of the field"—Ex. 23:16), this parable therefore illustrates by the twelve months of the year a period of gospel history, in the closing of which the kingdom of Christ is to be set up, and the beginning of which is

There being a period of church history illustrated by
this twelve month harvest

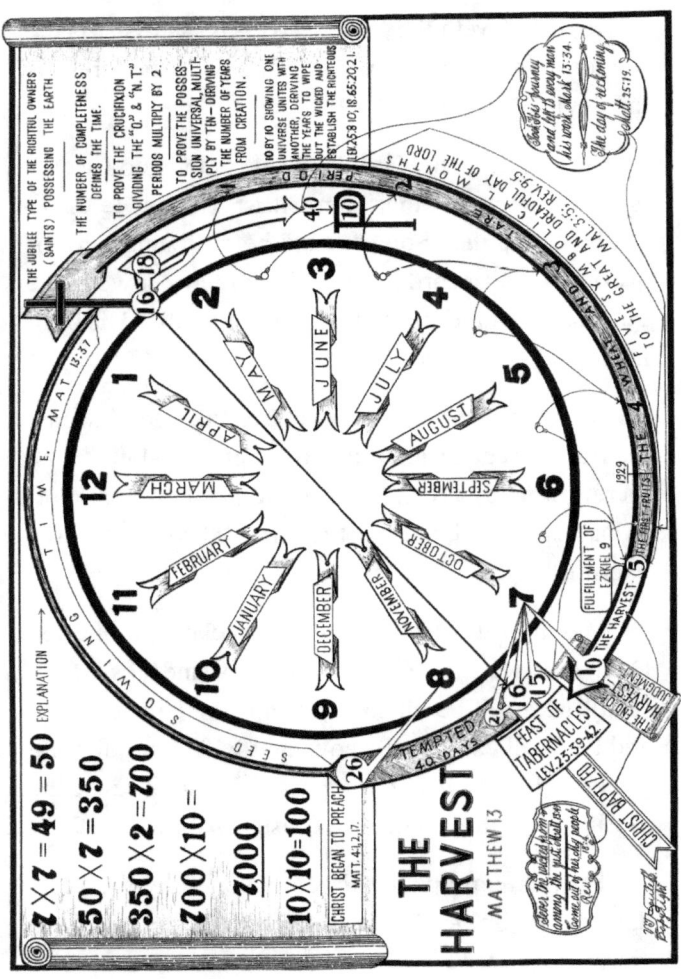

period, we must therefore find the time of its beginning—the time of seed-sowing, and the time of its closing—the time of reaping.

"He that soweth the good seed," says Christ, "is the Son of man," and the enemy that sowed the tares "is the devil." Matt. 13:37, 39.

"The Son of man," He who "soweth the good seed," is of course none other than Christ. But as He could not be called the "Son of *man*" before being born of a woman, He accordingly could not have sowed "the good seed" of the spiritual harvest until after His birth in Bethlehem, Judea.

As His ministry—His sowing of "the good seed," the truth—began right after His baptism (Matt. 4:17), therefore to establish the beginning of the parabolic harvest period, we must ascertain the date He was baptized.

"And after threescore and two weeks," prophesied Daniel, concerning Christ's ministry and His death, "shall Messiah be cut off, but not for Himself: . . . and He shall confirm the covenant with many for *one week*: and in the *midst of the week* He shall cause the sacrifice and the oblation to cease." Dan. 9:26, 27.

That this is prophetic time, reckoned by the year-day rule of Ezekiel 4:6, is seen from the fact that there were seven years from the time Christ was baptized to the time the apostles were permitted to take the gospel to the Gentiles. During this period, Christ confirmed or fulfilled the covenant. "In the midst of the week," or at the end of three and one half years, He was to be crucified, thus causing the earthly sacrifice to cease.

The fact having been established (see illustration in *The Shepherd's Rod*, Vol. 2, p. 22) that the three and one half years of Christ's ministry terminated on the *16th day* of the *first* month, then counting three and *one half* years (follow the illustration on p. 22), we find that His baptism took place on the 16th day of the *seventh* month which was in the Week of Tabernacles, and the celebration of which was the *end* of the agricultural year, the close of the harvest (Lev. 23:39).

Thus we see that the parable is in perfect fidelity to nature, and that "the Son of man" commenced sowing the spiritual seed right on time—in the end of the old and in the beginning of the new year's harvest—in precisely the right season of the year. With the sowing of the seed beginning with Christ's baptism, and the harvest coming at the "*end* of the *world*," the period of the parable obviously embraces the entire gospel dispensation—from the beginning of Christ's ministry to the close of probationary time. Between the two is the

Wheat-growing Time.

The three and one half years from the beginning of Christ's ministry to His crucifixion being the sowing time, and the harvest time being the end of the world, then the intervening period is the time for the growing and ripening of the grain, also the

Tare-sowing Time.

Upon finishing His sowing of the good seed, "the Son of man . . . left His house, and gave authority to His servants, and to every man his work, and commanded the porter to watch." Mark 13:34. But with Him gone, "men slept," as men are given to do when their employer is away. Thus, sometime after Christ ascended on high, "His enemy came and sowed tares among the wheat, and went his way." Matt. 13:25. But His servants, sleeping, knew it not! What a tragically ironic picture! Zion's watchmen fallen asleep on her very walls, while the enemy slips over unseen and unopposed! O what a fearful guilt of gross dereliction of duty lies upon the watchmen since apostolic days!

Denouncing those today responsible for this failure to protect the church from fellowshipping virtually anyone who professes an interest and shows a desire to be fellowshipped, though such a one neither be grounded in the truth nor bringing forth "fruits meet for repentance," the

Spirit of Prophecy declares: "Too much hasty work is done in adding names to the church roll. Serious defects are seen in the characters of some who join the church. Those who admit them say, We will first get them into the church, and then reform them. But this is a mistake. The very first work to be done is the work of reform. . . . *Do not* allow them to unite with God's people in church relationship until they have decided evidences that the Spirit of God is working upon their hearts. Many whose names are registered on the church books are not Christians."—*The Review and Herald*, May 21, 1901.

What stronger evidence is needed to convince oneself that the watchmen have lost the spiritual eyesight which John the Baptist and the apostles had? Tragically true indeed the sharp indictment: "Sleeping preachers preaching to a sleeping people."—*Testimonies*, Vol. 2, p. 337.

Discerning "when he saw many of the Pharisees and Sadducees come to his baptism," that they would later crucify his Lord, John said to them, "O generation of vipers who hath warned you to flee from the wrath to come? Bring forth therefore fruits meet for repentance." Matt. 3:7, 8. Thus he exposed and thwarted the devil's move to bring in the tares at that time. For well did he know that if the tares once got in and then he try to weed them out, he would uproot the wheat with them.

And then during the time of the apostles, Peter, as a faithful watchman of the church, detecting the devil's essaying again to come in with his bad seed, said to the guilty: "Ananias, why hath Satan filled thine heart to lie to the Holy Ghost, and to keep back part of the price of the land? . . . And Ananias hearing these words fell down, and gave up the ghost: and great fear came on all them that heard these things. . . . And it was about the space of three hours after, when his wife, . . . came in. And Peter answered unto her, Tell me whether ye sold the land for so much? And she said, Yea, for so much. . . . Then fell she down straightway at his feet, and yielded up the ghost." Acts, 5:3, 5, 7, 8, 10.

The fact that the congregation, too, has failed to discern the devil's sowing his seed among them, twice over vindicates the indictment: "Sleeping preachers, preaching to a *sleeping people*" (*Testimonies*, Vol. 2, p. 337), and proves that the entire church, both the ministry and the laity, is sound asleep, in fulfilment of the words of Christ: "Then shall the kingdom of heaven be likened unto ten virgins, . . . and five of them were wise, and five were foolish. . . . But . . . while the bridegroom tarried, *they all slumbered and slept.*" Matt. 25:1-5.

The evil of allowing the devil freely to sow the tares among the wheat, has existed in the Christian church since the passing of the apostles, with the result that whenever the Lord has sent a message to His people, the tares amongst them have straightway (at the instructions of the leaders) raised their hands and voted out whoever would listen to the messenger and obey the message. Thus time and again selling their birthright for less than a mess of pottage, the professed people of God have lost out, and still the church has never learned the tragic lesson!

"O ye house of Israel," warns the Lord, "let it suffice you of all your abominations, in that ye have brought into My sanctuary strangers, uncircumcised in heart, and uncircumcised in flesh, to be in My sanctuary, to pollute it, even My house." Ezek. 44:6, 7.

But ever to the faithful, as the tares have cast them out of their churches, the Lord's comforting assurance has been: "Blessed are ye when men shall hate you, and when they shall separate you from their company, and shall reproach you, and cast out your name as evil, for the Son of Man's sake. Rejoice ye in that day, and leap for joy: for, behold, your reward is great in heaven: for in the like manner did their fathers unto the prophets." Luke 6:22, 23.

As the period since the passing of the apostles has been the wheat- and tare-growing time, and as, moreover, the Laodicean church is the last of the seven sections of the Christian church in which are commingled the wheat and the tares, we must learn the answer to the question:

With Christendom become a veritable forest for the number of its denominations, sects, and cults, hence only by the omniscient Word of God can we pick out of it the Laodicean church.

The names of "the seven churches" (representing the successive sections of the Christian church, of which the Laodicean is the last) are not "just names." Take as a familiar example the name of the sixth, "Philadelphia." Its meaning, "brotherly love," being a misnomer of the spiritual condition of any other church organization in the entire Christian era, implicitly fits, however, the state of charity common and singular to the sixth—the Millerite church.

When the proclamation of the 2300 days of Daniel 8:14 sounded to the churches Prior to 1844, they arbitrarily denied their members the right of religious freedom, by forbidding them even to attend Miller's preaching, and by casting out those who accepted the message. Then after 1844 these same religious bodies opposed the preaching of the Three Angels' Messages (Rev. 14:6-11), again taking the same tyrannical actions against their free-minded brethren. The Millerite church by its actions in contrast to theirs, said," 'Let every man be fully persuaded in his own mind' (Rom. 14:5), and let us not interpose between God and His people by making

—62—

religious laws or by prohibiting the free exercise of any man's conscience."

Being the one shining example of a church never guilty of thwarting or trying to thwart in any way her members in their exercise of their inalienable right to investigate and to accept for themselves whatever their conscience bid them investigate and accept, she alone contributed nothing to the grievous condition calling forth the scripture: "Hear the Word of the Lord, ye that tremble at His word; your brethren that hated you, that cast you out for My name's sake, said, Let the Lord be glorified: but He shall appear to your joy, and they shall be ashamed" (Isa. 66:5) in the

Separation of the Tares
From Among the Wheat.

The end of the period in which the wheat and the tares are commingled is the time of the closing work for the Laodicean church (the last of the seven churches). This work is identified by the church's founder as the marking in Ezekiel 9, the sealing of spiritual Israel, the 144,000. (See *Testimonies to Ministers*, p. 445 and *Testimonies*, Vol. 3, p. 266; Vol. 5, p. 211.) And this identification is conclusively substantiated by the fact, as herein seen, that Ezekiel's prophecy is a separation of two classes—those who "sigh and cry for all the abominations that be done in the midst thereof" (the church) and those who do not. And as the former are delivered while the latter fall under the slaughter weapons of the angels, there is clearly seen a complete separation of the tares from among the wheat in the

Time of Harvest.

Though the true meaning and time of the harvest is greatly confused by some and confusing to many, a close study of the Word will clear it in just as simple manner as it cleared both the time of the seed-sowing and the period of the wheat and the tares.

With His eye piercing the mists of the ages, Christ foresaw the negligence of His watchmen and the evil which was to spring up in His church. Nevertheless, after being asked by His servants, "Didst not Thou sow good seed in Thy field? from whence then hath it tares? . . . Wilt Thou then that we go and gather them up? . . . He said, Nay; lest while ye gather up the tares, ye root up also the wheat with them. Let both grow together until the harvest: and *in the time* of harvest I will say to the reapers, Gather ye together first the tares, and bind them in bundles to burn them: but gather the wheat into My barn." Matt. 13:27-30.

A harvest means the "result of effort," of toil, "the gathering of a crop"—reaping the result of labor and filling up the barns with grain. So rather than the year's toil being finished at the beginning of the harvest, the heaviest labor of the year just then begins. And though harvest time is the shortest of all the periods of the harvest year, the work of reaping is not done in a moment; it takes time. The yield is not garnered by turning the field right into the barn; no, that would be a conglomerate mass instead of a harvest. First the sickle is put to the grain, and next the grain is bound into sheaves, then threshed, after which it is put into the barn; and thereafter the chaff and the tares are destroyed. This work being completed during the autumn, it shows that the harvest is a season of time after "the summer is past," and that it is followed by the fruitless winter period.

So it must be with the spiritual harvest, which otherwise could not be illustrated by the literal. Do not regard lightly the wisdom of God: His illustrations are perfect.

Consider, now, with what exact fidelity to the natural harvest the Master has stated the truths of the spiritual harvest: "Let both grow together until the harvest," He says: "and *in the time of* harvest I will say to the reapers, Gather ye together first the tares and bind them in bundles to burn them: but gather the wheat into My barn." Matt. 13:30.

In these parabolic words Christ has made the spiritual method of harvesting analogous to the natural method. Were the one not precisely like the other, He would have distinguished the difference. Be admonished, therefore, not to let vain imaginings come into the mind, but stand squarely on the Scriptures, for they are full of meaning of illimitable value—are, indeed, your very life.

As the word "until" means "up to," the tares are therefore to be gathered out, not before or after the harvest, but at the beginning of it. And "the time of harvest" being "the end of probationary time" (*Christ's Object Lessons*, p. 72), then the harvesting itself necessarily precedes the close of probation—the fruitless winter season. Consequently, the tares are separated from among the wheat before, not after, the end of probationary time.

The wheat, "the children of the kingdom" (verse 38), are gathered into the barn, the kingdom; the tares, "the children of the wicked one" (verse 38)—mere professors, those who are not doers of the Word, and who were granted membership "while men slept"—"are gathered and burned in the fire" (verse 40), after the wheat is bound into sheaves. But

Who Are the Reapers?

"The reapers are the angels" who "shall come forth, and sever the wicked from among the just." Matt. 13:39, 49. These angels are not those who shall "come" with Christ at His second coming, but rather those whom He "shall send forth." They are like the three angels of Revelation 14:6-11. Indeed, the third angel "is to select the wheat from the tares and seal, or bind, the wheat for the heavenly garner."—*Early Writings*, p. 118. Therefore the angels, the reapers, whom Christ sends forth, include both him who does the sealing, or binding, and those who follow on to do the destroying (Ezek. 9:2, 5, 6), first in the church, then in the world. Thus is the

Separation in Two Sections.

The command, "Gather out of His kingdom all things that offend, and them which do iniquity," does not mean to gather His saints from the earth into heaven; neither does it mean to destroy the wicked from the earth; for the former are to be gathered, not directly to heaven, but first into "the barn," the kingdom on earth; and the latter are not to be destroyed immediately "in the time of harvest," but first are to be gathered into bundles, and then destroyed, as is further illustrated in the parable of the net:

"Again, the kingdom of heaven is like unto a net, that was cast into the sea, and gathered of every kind: which, when it was full, they drew to shore, and sat down, and gathered the good into vessels, but cast the bad away." Matt. 13:47, 48.

This parable also shows the separation of the wicked from among God's people in the church ("the net"), this being the first section of the work of separation, the beginning of the harvest. The subsequent section follows in the world, as the earth is lightened with the glory of the "Loud Cry" angel, and as "another voice from heaven," says: "Come out of her, My people, that ye be not partakers of her sins, and that ye receive not of her plagues." Rev. 18:4.

Note that in the first section of the separation, the one in the church, the wicked are taken away from among the just, whereas in the second, the one in Babylon, the just are *called* from *among* the wicked.

As the field is "the world" (Matt. 13:38), the parable of the wheat and the tares necessarily comprehends both sections of the harvest. As, by contrast, the "net" hauls in the "fish," the converts made by the gospel church, the parable of the net therefore is limited to the separation in the church. Together they distinguish the

Relation of First Fruits to Second.

Isaiah also was given a view of this twofold harvest. "For by fire and by His sword," he prophesies, "will the Lord plead with all flesh: and the slain of the Lord shall be many. They that sanctify themselves, and purify themselves in the gardens behind one tree in the midst, eating swine's flesh, and the abomination, and the mouse, shall be consumed together, saith the Lord." Isa. 66:16, 17.

The *slain* of the Lord, in this scripture, are those who profess to be in the faith, who claim sanctification and purification, but who do so on the merits of their own righteousness,—of "themselves",—not on the merits of Christ's righteousness. They walk, that is, in their own ways, not in obedience to the truth. Wrapped about with these spurious habiliments of sanctification and purification, they pose as reformers, yet all the while indulging in the abominations of the heathen; doing so in secret—"behind one tree," or, as the margin says, following in the lead "one after another." And the food (swine's flesh, the mouse, and the abomination,—whatever that may be wherever these paganistic Christians may be,—foods used respectively only in certain parts of the world, among different classes and races) with which they are gratifying their appetites, shows that the consequent destruction among these self-sanctified and self-purified ones is in the church world-wide.

That it was not among the Gentiles, who knew not of the truth of God and of His great power is clearly shown by the Lord's words: "I will send those *that escape of them* unto the nations, to Tarshish, Pul, and Lud, that draw the bow, to Tubal, and

Javan [the Gentile nations today as called by their ancient names], to the isles afar off, that *have not* heard My fame, *neither have seen My glory*; and *they shall* declare My glory among the Gentiles." Isa. 66:19.

Since these escaped ones (the first fruits, the 144,000 servants of God—Rev.7:3) "shall bring *all* your brethren" (the second fruits, the great multitude—Rev. 7:9) "for an offering . . . *out of all Nations*" (Isa. 66:20, first part), this great ingathering necessarily, therefore, is the closing work of the gospel—the second section of the harvest.

And since, furthermore, these escaped ones are to bring all their brethren "to My holy mountain Jerusalem, saith the Lord," "in a *clean vessel* into the house of the Lord" (verse 20, last part), the fact is fully evident that the destruction of the wicked results in the purification of the church. The "clean vessel" is therefore the purified church, composed of the escaped ones—the first fruits, the 144,000—who, free from the wicked (the tares) shall then, as "the servants of our God," bring in the second fruits, the great multitude which no man can number, out of all nations.

The second section of the separation thus being completed, probationary time is closed. Whereupon from the wicked will be heard the horrible wail of doom: "The harvest is past, the summer is ended, and we are not saved." Jer. 8:20.

This being the dreadful experience of the tares in Babylon, in the second section of the harvest, there must, as a type, be a similar and precedent experience for the tares in the Laodicean church, in the first section of the harvest, a parallel which shows conclusively that

The Church Is Not Babylon.

The reason that the church is figuratively *not* "Babylon" is that it is called Jerusalem (Ezek. 9:4, 8), and from among the good therein, the *wicked* (the tares) are destroyed, *taken out*, by the six men with the slaughter weapons (Ezek. 9:6-9), and then afterward the good (the wheat) are gathered in "the barn"; while from among the wicked in Babylon, the *just* ("My people") are called *out* and gathered into the barn, and then the remaining wicked are destroyed by the *seven angels'* pouring out the seven last plagues.

Thus in the first section of the harvest, the separation in the church, the wicked are destroyed by *six men* with slaughter weapons, *before* the good are *taken* out; and in the second section, the separation among the churches in Babylon, the wicked are destroyed by *seven* angels with the seven last plagues, *after* the good are taken out. There are therefore two separations and two fruits: the former gives the first fruits, the 144,000, who are not defiled with women (Rev. 14:4). That is, they are those whom the sealing message finds in the church of God, not in the heathen churches. And the second gives the second fruits, the great multitude from all nations, some of whom also may be undefiled with women—heathen churches.

Having to this point studied the judgment, the harvest, in the light of the testimonies of the prophets and the parables of Christ, we shall now examine it

In the Light of the Ceremonial Service.

Just as the Spirit of Prophecy declares that "the whole system of types and symbols was a compacted prophecy of the gospel, a presentation in which were bound up the promises of redemption" (*The Acts of the Apostles*, p. 14), just so the plan of salvation is unfolded not only in the testimonies of the prophets and in the parables of Christ but also in the types and symbols of the earthly sanctuary. In addition to this, the experiences of the people in the typical period "happened unto them," we are told, "for ensamples: and they are written for our admonition, upon whom the ends of the world are come." 1 Cor. 10:11. So we are logically bound at the very outset to attend to God's instruction to Moses:

"On the tenth day of this seventh month there shall be a day of atonement: . . . make an atonement for you before the

Lord your God. For whatsoever soul it be that shall not be afflicted in that same day, he shall be cut off from among his people." "Make an atonement for the children of Israel . . . once a year." Lev. 23:27-29; 16:34.

When one is "cut off from among his people" on account of sin, then his name must also be "blotted out of the book of the living." Ps. 69:28. Consequently, the day of atonement was a day of judgment, as it is still commonly called by the Jews, and by that token it was founded as the type of the great antitypical day of atonement (the investigative judgment)—the day in which the Lord will blot from His book the names of all sinners, and "cut off" from the congregation of His people all whose names are not in the book.

Concerning the typical day of atonement, the Lord's command through Moses was: "*On that day* shall the priest make an atonement for you, to cleanse you, that ye may be *clean from all your sins before the Lord. . . . and he shall make an atonement for the holy sanctuary, and he shall make an atonement for the tabernacle of the congregation, and for the altar.*" Lev. 16:30, 33.

Being the day of atonement in type for both the dead and the living, this service of the earthly tabernacle therefore projects the day of atonement in its antitype—the cleansing of the sanctuary in heaven from unworthy names in the books, and the cleansing of the church on earth from its unconverted and unstable members,—thus bringing the time of clean books, clean church, and clean people.

Looking forward to this day of purification, Zechariah prophesies: "*In that day* shall there be upon the horses, HOLINESS UNTO THE LORD; and the pots in the Lord's house shall be like the bowls before the altar. Yea, every pot in Jerusalem and in Judah shall be holiness unto the Lord of hosts: . . . and *in that day* there shall be *no more* the Canaanite in the house of the Lord of hosts." Zech. 14:20, 21.

Envisioning the same scene, the prophet Isaiah declares: "And the Gentiles shall see thy righteousness, and *all kings* thy glory: and thou shalt be called by a *new name*, which the mouth of the Lord shall name. Thou shalt also be a crown of glory in the hand of the Lord, and a royal diadem in the hand of thy God. Thou shalt no more be termed Forsaken; . . . thou shalt be called Hephzibah . . . *The holy people*." Isa. 62:2-4, 12.

"But ye . . . that forsake the Lord, that forget My holy mountain, . . . ye shall leave your name for a curse unto *My chosen*: for the Lord God shall slay thee, and call His servants by another name." Isa. 65:11, 15.

"The people that doth not understand shall fall." Hos. 4:14. "Many shall be purified, and made white, and tried; but the wicked shall do wickedly: and none of the wicked shall understand; but the wise shall understand." Dan. 12:10.

Those whose vision is clear on the truth of the harvest as taught in the testimonies of the prophets and in the parables will have a still clearer vision as we study the significance of

The Wave-Sheaf, Wave-Loaves, and the Feast of Tabernacles.

Illustrating our salvation in completeness, the harvest rites of the ceremonial system must therefore corroborate both the testimonies of the prophets and the parables concerning the harvest, for all are inextricably bound up together. The ceremonies of the first and the second fruits of grain must accordingly unfold the truth concerning the first and second fruits of humanity. In the Levitical law we read:

"Ye shall bring a *sheaf of the firstfruits* of your harvest unto the priest: and he shall wave the sheaf before the Lord, to be accepted for you: on the morrow after the Sabbath the priest shall wave it. . . . And ye shall eat neither bread, nor parched corn, nor green ears, until the selfsame day that ye have brought an offering unto your God: . . . and ye shall count unto you from the morrow after the Sabbath, from the day that ye brought the sheaf of the wave offering; seven Sabbaths shall be complete:

—75—

even unto the morrow after the seventh Sabbath shall ye number fifty days; and ye shall offer a new meat offering unto the Lord. Ye shall bring out of your habitations *two wave loaves* of two tenth deals: they shall be of fine flour; they shall be baken with leaven; they are the first fruits unto the Lord. . . . Also in the fifteenth day of the seventh month, when ye have *gathered in the fruit of the land*, ye shall keep a feast unto the Lord *seven days:* on the first day shall be a sabbath, and on the eighth day shall be a sabbath." Lev. 23:10, 11, 14-17, 39.

Here we see commanded the observance of three harvest rites: (1) the ceremony of the wave-sheaf, at the beginning of the first harvest; (2) the ceremony of the wave-loaves, at the close of the first harvest; and (3) the feast of tabernacles, at the close of the second harvest. Being typical, these two grain harvests with their three literal sacraments, accordingly foreshadow two soul harvests with three spiritual rites, the first of which is the

First Fruits with Wave-Sheaf and Wave-Loaves.

Being of cut stalks of grain, the wave-sheaf signified fruits to be harvested. And as the sheaf was to be offered before the sickle was put to the grain and gathered into sheaves, it obviously pointed forward to a spiritual harvest of first fruits to be gathered.

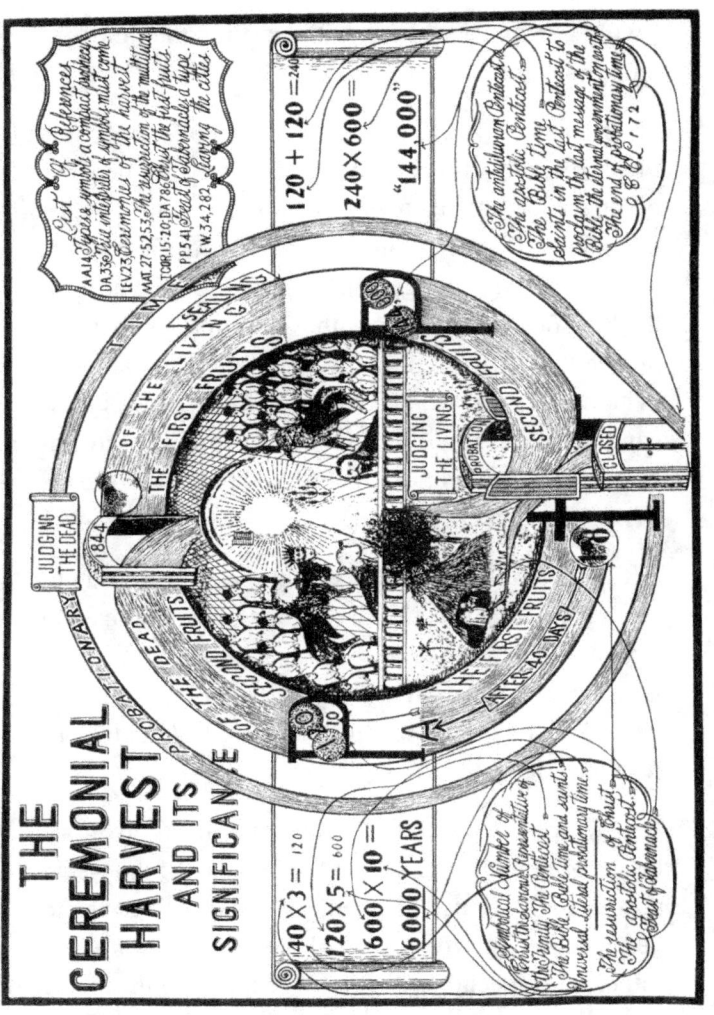

On Pentecost, fifty days after the typical sheaf was offered, all Israel were to offer "a new meat offering unto the Lord . . .

[two wave-loaves "baken with leaven"] the firstfruits unto the Lord." Lev. 23:16, 17.

Both the wave-sheaf and the wave-loaves were thank offerings for the first fruits. One was dedicated at the beginning of the harvest; the other at the completion of it. In contrast to the *wave-sheaf* of *cut stalks* of grain, prefiguring fruits to be gathered after the sheaf was offered, the *wave-loaves*, being a *finished product*, signified fruits previously gathered. (The reader who would best comprehend the significance of these three ceremonial celebrations all-important to our salvation, will follow the chart of page 77, as we proceed.)

It will be observed that the command regarding observance of the seventh-day Sabbath, as well as that regarding observance of the yearly ceremonial feasts, is recorded in the twenty-third chapter of Leviticus, verse 3. Care, therefore, must be exercised not to confuse the one truth with the other.

The wave-sheaf was to be offered "on the morrow after the Sabbath"—that is, on the first day of the week, now commonly called Sunday. This offering was to be presented, not on a special day of the month, but rather on a special day of the week, before the sickle was put to the grain and gathered into sheaves (Lev. 23:11, 14). Coming just at the right time, in the season of the first fruits, the Passover

—78—

week was the period in which the wave-sheaf was usually offered before the Lord, its ritual prophetically projecting

Christ, the Antitype of the Wave-Sheaf.

For more than a thousand years the annual waving of the sheaf pointed forward to its antitypical event, the resurrection of Christ. And as Christ arose on the very day that the wave-sheaf was to be offered, the day "after the Sabbath," let no one attribute the singular concurrence of these two events on that day to mere coincidence or to any cause other than divine design. "He was the antitype of the wave-sheaf," declares the Spirit of Prophecy, "and His resurrection took place on the very day when the wave-sheaf was to be presented before the Lord."—*Desire of Ages*, p. 785.

So Christ, the first fruits, and those who with Him at His resurrection came forth from the grave, raised to everlasting life, were the antitypical wave-sheaf of the dead. And since the wave-sheaf of grain pointed forward to the ingathering of the first fruits of the field, just so those who arose with Christ, being first fruits of the dead, pointed forward to the ingathering of the gospel's first fruits—the 120 disciples. But as those who arose with Christ ascended with Him as trophies of His victory over death and the grave, they thereby became a living type, and thus

The Wave-Sheaf of the Living.

Just as Christ arose on the very day the sheaf was to be offered, likewise the Holy Spirit fell upon the 120 disciples on the very day the wave-loaves were to be presented before the Lord. The apostolic Pentecost was accordingly the prototype of the ceremonial Pentecost (the day the wave-loaves were offered). And since the wave-sheaf was a figure of Christ and of those who arose with Him as the first of the first fruits of the dead, hence the wave-loaves were a figure of the 120 Spirit-filled disciples who were the full complement of first fruits of the dead, and who were gathered in after the resurrection.

From these facts it can more clearly be seen that those whom Christ took with Him were the living wave-sheaf and the only one that has been offered in the heavenly sanctuary; and that as ones raised from the dead, they are the first fruits of the dead, whereas as ones everliving before the Father, they are the living wave-sheaf of the first fruits of the living, the 144,000 servants of God, who sequentially precede

The Second Fruits and the Feast of Tabernacles.

The 120 disciples on the day of Pente-cost being the gospel's first fruits of the dead, it follows that the great multitude added to the church daily thereafter, naturally were the gospel's second fruits of the dead.

"Also in the fifteenth day of the seventh month," continues the Levitical record of the Lord's commands concerning the harvest rites, "when ye have gathered in the fruit of the land, ye shall keep a feast unto the Lord seven days: . . . and ye shall take you on the first day the boughs of goodly trees, branches of palm trees, and the boughs of thick trees, and willows of the brook; and ye shall rejoice before the Lord your God seven days. . . . Ye shall dwell in booths seven days; all that are Israelites born shall dwell in booths." Lev. 23:39, 40, 42.

As the wave-sheaf and the wave-loaves are typical, then also the Feast of Tabernacles must be typical. Otherwise the ceremony would not have been observed as a part of the harvest rite. And as in the type the feast was to be celebrated at the close of the final ingathering of the year's harvest, then correspondingly in the antitype it must be celebrated at the close of the final ingathering of earth's harvest, which is nearing its fulfillment. So the time consumed in producing and in offering the wave-sheaf and the wave-loaves, also in observing the Feast of Tabernacles, is representative of the entire spiritual harvest time of the living and of the dead.

Bearing out this fact the Spirit of Prophecy says:

"The Feast of Tabernacles was not only commemorative, but typical. . . . It celebrated the ingathering of the fruits of the earth, and *pointed forward to the great day of final ingathering*, when the Lord of the *harvest shall send forth His reapers* to gather the tares together in bundles for the fire, and *to gather the wheat into His garner*. At that time the wicked will all be destroyed."—*Patriarchs and Prophets*, p. 541.

Plainly, therefore, since the first and the second fruits of the literal harvest and its attendant rites foreshadowed a spiritual harvest of first and second fruits, they are to be climaxed by the antitypical Feast of Tabernacles.

"I saw the saints," says the servant of the Lord in describing this celebration, "leaving the cities and villages, and associating together in companies, and living in the most solitary places. Angels provided them food and water, while the wicked were suffering from hunger and thirst."—*Early Writings*, p. 282.

Thus ancient Israel's dwelling in booths typifies modern Israel's eventually dwelling in the woods. Irrefutably, therefore, the harvest of Matthew 13 precedes the close of probation, and is the time of the ingathering of the first and second fruits—the 144,000 and the "great multitude",—all the saints who are to be translated.

As the light focusing to this point clearly reveals that the Pentecost after the resurrection was for the ingathering of those who were to die, there must, correspondingly, be a Pentecost for the ingathering of those who are to be translated. And by the same token of logic, the wave-sheaf and the wave-loaves must have a double application, each to the dead and to the living, together comprising the total fruits of the antitypical harvest.

The apostolic Pentecost in providing the power for the ingathering of second fruits up to the beginning of the judgment of those who are now dead, foretokened the final Pentecost, which is yet future, and which is to bring the power for the ingathering of the second fruits of the living, those who shall never die. In other words, those who died prior to the final Pentecost are to be judged by the light of truth reflected through the power of the apostolic Pentecost.

(From His baptism to His ascension, Christ taught abroad the truth which was to prepare those who accepted it, to impart it. Then on the day of Pentecost, He endued them with His Spirit to proclaim it with power.)

Concerning the judgment, the harvest, the servant of the Lord declares:

"I then saw the third angel. Said my accompanying angel, 'Fearful is his work. Awful is his mission. He is the angel that is to select the wheat from the tares, and

seal, or bind, the wheat for the heavenly garner.' "—
Early Writings, p. 118.

"Now therefore be ye not mockers, lest your bands be made strong: for I have heard from the Lord God of hosts a consumption, even determined upon the whole earth. Give ye ear, and hear My voice; hearken, and hear My speech." Isa. 28:22, 23.

And now that each one who honestly seeks to hear and to heed the voice of Truth may have the clearest possible grasp of the several aspects of the subject of the judgment, the harvest, they are hereat brought into consolidated focus:

The reader will remember that those who arose with Christ on the eighteenth day of the first month (follow the chart on page 55), were immortalized and received into heaven as the antitypical sheaf, pointing to the ingathering of the fruits that shall never die. Their resurrection from the dead signified the beginning of the first-fruit harvest of the 120 disciples who were to die and be resurrected. The fact that the followers of Christ were not of one accord before the resurrection, is very positive testimony that the first fruits (the 120) of them that sleep did not ripen (become fully converted) until after the resurrection.

The 40 days of Christ's personal presence on earth after His resurrection was the time in which the first fruits were gathered in, for after His ascension the Christians closeted themselves in the upper room and did not emerge to preach the truth until the Pentecost. The 120, who received the power of the Spirit on the very day the wave-loaves were offered, were therefore the antitypical wave-loaves, signifying the completeness of the first fruit harvest. Subsequently came the second fruits of the dead, in the period of which the tares were commingled with the wheat.

Wonderful indeed is the way in which God has worked out the plan of salvation and revealed it step by step as necessary. When in 1844 the investigative judgment of the dead and the ingathering of the first fruits of the living began, He did not leave His people in darkness concerning these events. The very first vision which Sister White received in 1844 was of the 144,000 first fruits, the "servants of our God," who shall never taste death. (See *Early Writings*, pp. 13-15.)

Just as Christ and those whom He raised and took with Him became the prototypical sheaf, betokening the ingathering of the first fruits (the 120) of those who are to be resurrected, so also when He entered upon His priestly ministration in the first apartment of the heavenly sanctuary, and presented Himself and His trophies before His Father, they became the antitypical sheaf, betokening the ingathering of the first fruits of those who are to be translated (the 144,000 living saints). In the light of this parallel, the spiritual condition of the 120 before the apostolic Pentecost is clearly seen to typify the spiritual condition of the 144,000 before the future Pentecost.

The 40 days (Acts 1:3, 9) from the resurrection to the ascension are consequently typical of the period from 1844 to the fulfilment of the marking and slaying as recorded in Ezekiel 9 and Revelation 7:3-8; 14:1-5 respectively, and in *Testimonies to Ministers*, p. 445, *Testimonies*, Vol. 3, p. 266, also *Early Writings*, pp. 270-273.

After the first fruits are sealed and the tares are removed from among them, they then being separate from the influence of the world, as were the 120 on the day of Pentecost, will receive the outpouring of "the Holy Spirit in as much greater measure, as the increase of wickedness demands a more decided call to repentance."—*Testimonies*, Vol. 7, p. 33.

The first fruits of the dead (120) being a numbered company, and the second fruits of the dead (the multitudes gathered after Pentecost) being an unnumbered company, so correspondingly must it be with first and second fruits of the living. Hence the sealing of the 144,000 first fruits; and hence "after this," says John, "I beheld, and, lo, a great multitude, *which no man could number*, of all nations, and kindreds, and people, and tongues, stood before the throne, and before the Lamb, clothed with white robes, and palms in their hands . . . and all the angels stood round about the throne, and about the elders and the four beasts." Rev. 7:9, 11.

Mark carefully that this great multitude stood before the throne, not bodily, but figuratively only, as viewed in *Early Writings*, p. 55, and as is evidenced by the twofold fact that (1) the angels "stood round about the throne and about the elders and the four beasts," showing that the great multitude was *outside* the angelic circle; and that (2) the presence of the angels, the elders, and the four beasts about the throne shows that the judgment (Rev. 4:2-6) was still in session, and that therefore probation had not closed.

The palms in the hands of the great multitude (Rev. 7:9, 11), and the "victor's palm" placed "in every hand" of "the unnumbered host of the redeemed" (*The Great Controversy*, p. 646), betoken two entirely different events: for the latter received both a "victor's *palm* and [a] shining *harp*," whereas the former had no harps but *only palms*. "The unnumbered host of the redeemed" received their palms and harps in heaven, upon ascending in the "cloudy chariot," and just before entering the holy city. The great multitude, though, had their palms on earth, for, as we have seen, they had them during the time of the investigative judgment in the heavenly sanctuary—before the close of probation. (See Revelation 4 and 5; *The Shepherd's Rod*, Vol. 2, pp. 194-197.)

Clearly, then, while the palms and the harps of the redeemed hosts in heaven are *actual* guerdons of victory, the palms of the great multitude on the earth are *figurative* victory-palms.

Having thus far studied the harvest in the light of the testimonies of the prophets, the parables, and the ceremonies, we are now led to view it

In the Light of Number.

Though the wicked are swept along by a current from which they can no more escape than they can stem or resist, yet they can neither see it nor understand it, for the Word *alone* thus enlightens and enpowers the soul. Blessed indeed is the man who makes It a lamp to his feet, and a light to his path (Ps. 119:105). Brother, Sister, is It in dark parables to you? Your answer will tell you whether you are of those who walk in the light or of those who stumble in the darkness, and only a right relation to God can secure you to the one class and keep you out of the other.

If you think that Christ undesignedly remained 40 days after the resurrection, or that the Holy Ghost fell on the 120 just because there happened to be that many; or that purely by chance 12,000 out of each tribe are to be sealed; then you might just as well think that the fact that 12 times 12,000 equals 144,000 is a mathematical accident! Just what you think will give you the measure of the light there is in you.

"The words that I speak unto you, . . . they are *life*." John 6:63.

"Man shall not live by bread alone, but by *every* word of God." Luke 4:4.

As number is the natural mode of time equations, the Scriptures often therefore employ it to reveal the length of time from one Biblical event to another. Thus, time from the waving of the sheaf of first fruits to the Pentecost is equated by multiplying the number of days (7) allotted to the first of the harvest ceremonies, the feast of unleavened bread, by the number of weeks (7) to the Pentecost, which is 7x7, or 49 days. Similarly, the duration from one Jubilee to another is found by multiplying the number of years making a sabbatical year (7) by 7 sabbatical years, giving 7x7, or 49 years. Very obviously, then, the Scriptures commonly employ the process of multiplication in Their revealing of the truth.

Doubtless to some, these numerical equations will seem strange—as strange as the thought of the earth's revolving on its axis was to the world of the Dark Ages! It is the incredibilities of today, however, that are the taken-for-granted realities of tomorrow. So, though at present time little do we know of the many Bible numerics and their veiled code of truth, not so is it always to be, for God has placed them along the Bible's highways and byways of Truth, as signposts calculated to point and to illuminate the Royal Road to the Kingdom. So may every traveler thereon rejoice in deep gratitude for every ray of truth lighting his way. May the Lord forbid that any take the least chance in the darkness. And may each from unfeigning lips cry unto Heaven: "O send out Thy light and Thy truth: let them lead me; let them bring me unto Thy holy hill, and to Thy tabernacles" (Ps. 43:3), that I may "be filled with the knowledge of the glory of the Lord" (Hab. 2:14), yea even to the knowledge of

The Number of the Saviour.

The fact that Christ after the resurrection remained with His disciples just 40 days, not more or less, is no mere happenstance lightly to be brushed aside. Obviously an integral part of the over-all pattern of revealed truth, it is to be reckoned with accordingly. And since its modality is numerical, the entire subject involved must be explored in number, and the results equated in numerical values.

The Lord being the visible representative

of the Father, Son, and Holy Ghost, then the number of His personal office (3) and the number of days (40) of His personal supervision in the ingathering of His people must, in right equation, reveal Him as the Saviour of His people in the Old Testament period as well as in the New.

As the ingathering (40) through His personal presence (3) resulted in the outpouring of the Holy Spirit, the two must in right relation reveal

The Number of Saints on the Pentecost.

The product of Christ's ingathering through His personal presence being the first fruits up to the Pentecost, then it follows as a logical sequence that the product of the number of the gathering time (40) and the number of His person (3), must give the actual number of saints there were on the day of Pentecost. The equation, 40x3, giving 120, exactly numbers the first fruits to receive the Holy Spirit at that time!

Thus being as they were the product of the omnipotent power of the three persons of the Godhead (the Father, the Son, and the Holy Ghost) at work for 40 days through the personal ministry of their triune representative, Christ, this preternatural little group consequently preserved and continued the line of the church.

When reduced to its primary significance,

this succession of numerical facts leads to the conclusion that 3, the number of the Father, Son, and Holy Ghost, is therefore numerically figurative of the Trinity, and that 120, the number of the Father, Son, Holy Ghost times the number of the saints, is therefore numerically figurative of the Pentecost—a basic factor in the equation of salvation, and one inseparably linked to the relation of

Christ and the Bible.

It was to Christ in both of His forms that John alluded in his declarations: "That which was *from the beginning*, which we have *heard*, which we have *seen* with our eyes, which we have *looked* upon, and our hands have *handled*, of the Word of life." 1 John 1:1. "And the *Word* was made *flesh*," he further declares, "and dwelt among us, (and we beheld His glory, the glory as of the only begotten of the Father,) full of grace and truth." John 1:14.

Christ is the Word incarnate; the Bible, the Word written; or, to put it still more specifically, the Bible is Christ in the form of words, and Christ is the Bible in the form of man. Hence it follows that as Christ in the flesh is identified by a number, so must Christ in the Word. And therefore next to be ascertained is the

Number of the Bible.

The parable of the eleventh-hour call (Matthew 20) reveals that the Bible contains just 5 time-messages; the first "early in the morning," the second at the "the third hour," The third at the "the sixth and ninth hour," and the fifth at "the eleventh hour"; 5 in all. In these 5 parabolical calls are found all the time-messages called for in the Bible from the time that It (the Light of the world) began to come up (be written), early in the morning of the parabolical period, to its end—the twelfth hour. In other words, when these 5 messages have been proclaimed to the world, the Bible will then be an exhausted book so far as its offering any more salvation is concerned. (For full treatment of Matthew 20, see *The Shepherd's Rod*, Vol. 2, pp. 222-238.)

There being, then, just 5 messages of salvation in the Bible, the number of the Bible can only be 5, with the next step being to find the

Number of Bible Ingathering Time.

Since this number is to designate the time of ingathering of saints, therefore we must multiply the number of the saints on Pentecost (120) by the number of the Bible (5), the product of which is 600. Accordingly, 600 is the number of the Bible's ingathering time—a period which as a factor in our equation leads on sequentially to the

Number of Years Christ Is a Saviour.

Let the fact be kept well in mind that we

are at present exploring number for the truth that Christ is the Saviour of the world before and during Bible times. So obviously our aim is to find, not the number of the saints that Christ is to save, but the number of years He will be a Saviour. Hence, we here remind the reader that the parabolical calls, or messages, of Matthew 20 embrace only a part of church history; specifically, that part from the time that Moses began to write the Bible, from the time of the "Exodus," to probation's close. But as Christ is the Redeemer of the world before as well as after the advent of the Bible, the equation under discussion must consequently embrace the entire span of probationary time since the day Adam sinned. This demands therefore that the number of probationary time, 600, the multiplicand, be multiplied by a multiplier having universal value, to show that Christ is the only Saviour in all ages.

Number 10 is by universal admission the Biblical number of universal value. In the great image of Daniel 2, the 10 toes symbolize the world at the second coming of Christ. Then in the so-called non-descript beast (Daniel 7), the leopard-like beast (Rev. 13:1-10), and the scarlet-colored beast (Rev. 17:1-3), the 10 horns depict the world's kingdoms at different times. While on the other side of the picture, the 10 virgins represent the entire membership of the church world-wide. (For further treatment of these values, see

The Shepherd's Rod, Vol. 2, pp. 84-125.)

Clearly, therefore, the universal number by which we must multiply the number of probationary time (600) is 10, and 600x10 gives 6,000. Here at long last is the consummate vindication of the Christian's belief that the years of human probation are 6,000! Here, in other words, is proof in the absolute that when the angel of mercy soon finally folds her wings and takes her flight forever from this world of sin, earth and its beings under sin will have been in existence for 6,000 years! Then comes the millennium, the 1,000 years in which Satan is bound and the wicked are judged (Rev. 20:3, 12).

Thus in the eternal drama, the strange interlude of sin and redemption runs for 7,000 years (perfect completeness), or but one short week out of eternity, as it were with the Lord, 1000 years being as a day with Him (2 Pet. 3:8). Strange interlude indeed! The Mystery of Godliness in mysterious sufferance of the mystery of iniquity! Mystery of mysteries! Wondrous, unfathomable love of God to man!

What awful solemnity invests this momentous mathematical demonstration of the great gospel truths! Revealing as it does that Christ is the only Redeemer of the world and in all ages, its truth perfectly bears out the scripture: ". . . there is none other name under heaven given among men, whereby we must be saved."

Acts 4:12. And at the same time it serves warning that we are living in the last days of probation, "the time of the end," the time of the harvest.

Having brought us to the time of the harvest of the living, to the last days of the 6,000 years of human probation, the equation must, to be complete, include the number of

The Numbered Living Saints.

The apostolic Pentecost, it is to be noted, did not completely fulfill the prophetic Pentecost of Joel 2:28, 32, a prophecy specifically of the last days, although Peter did refer to the scripture in his Pentecostal sermon (Acts 2:14-21). And surest evidence that the prophecy is yet to be fulfilled is that the apostolic Pentecost is the prototype of the latter day, the antitypical, Pentecost—that which is just ahead of us.

Since the church on earth has had three dispensations, the Noatic, the Abrahamic, and the Christian, and since both the Abrahamic and the Christian dispensations closed with a Pentecost, as previously mentioned, necessarily, then, so likewise must have closed the Noatic dispensation. Otherwise, Noah's message would have lacked power and light to show the Way of Life to that "evil and adulterous generation," and as a consequence God could not justly have destroyed them by the flood.

Peter himself understood that there was

an antediluvian Pentecost. This he very definitely testifies in the statement: "For Christ . . . being put to death in the flesh, but *quickened by the Spirit: by which also He went* and *preached* unto the spirits in prison; which sometime were disobedient, *when* once the longsuffering of God waited *in the days of Noah, while the ark was a preparing.*" 1 Pet. 3:18-20.

In Peter's statement, Inspiration records that the same Spirit Who quickened Christ, preached to the antediluvians while they were in prison—in chains of circumstance which in their wickedness and rejection of truth they blindly forged and bound upon themselves, and from which they could find no escape save through the ark that was "a preparing." And the ark, they would not enter. Thus they were left without hope and without an excuse.

Plainly, then, there are three Pentecosts to be reckoned with in the equation of salvation: two in the past and one in the future, the first being the type, the second the prototype, the third the antitype. Or, in other words, the first brought the earnest of the establishment of the church, the second the foundation of the church (Rev. 21:14), and the third will bring its completion and glorification. The second, the apostolic Pentecost, being the foundational one, also the only one historically recorded, it is therefore the lightbearer on the subject; showing that in order for the antediluvian world to be benefited by redemption, the Noatic Pentecost was indispensable and must therefore be accounted for in this numerical study.

The number of the saints from the one on record being 120, it follows that the combined number of the two must be 120 plus 120, or 240, as illustrated on page 77.

Remember that these numbers do not determine how many are saved in each, but how many receive the Pentecostal power.

There remains now but to ascertain the number of saints to receive the third and last Pentecost, and to do so the number of the two Pentecosts (240) need only be multiplied by the number of the Bible ingathering time (600), making 600x240, which gives 144,000, the very number prophesied!

Thus struck in the rock of truth forever is the number of the recipients of the great Pentecost just ahead of us, the number of the first fruits of those who are to be translated, 144,000 guileless (Rev. 14:5) "servants of our God." Rev. 7:3. In the pure and full power of the Spirit, proclaiming the pure and full gospel unto all the nations, they "go forth conquering and to conquer" (*Prophets and Kings*, p. 725), and "bring all [their] brethren for an offering unto the Lord out of all nations upon horses, and in chariots, and in litters, and upon mules, and upon swift beasts, to My holy mountain Jerusalem, saith the Lord, as the children of Israel bring an offering *in a clean vessel into the house of the Lord.*" Isa. 66:20. "And then shall the end come." Matt. 24:14.

Thus thrillingly unfolded in number, the absolute mode of truth, is the equation of salvation, out of which, just briefly to recapitulate, emerges the number of Christ as representative of the Godhead on earth, 3; the number of the gathering time, 40; the number of the saints in the apostolic Pentecost, 120; the combined number of the saints in the Noatic and the apostolic Pentecost, 240; the number of the Bible, 5; the number of the Bible ingathering time, 600; the number of recipients of the final Pentecost, 144,000; the number of the entire period of human probation, 6,000; and finally, the number of the overall time of sin and redemption, 7,000. What priceless Gift divine! And O may this realization stir the heart of every earnest reader, as it did the heart of David, to give praise and thanksgiving to God for His inexpressible love to man: "O Lord," sings the prophet, "Thou art my God; I will exalt Thee, I will praise Thy name; for Thou has done wonderful things; Thy counsels of old are faithfulness and truth." Isa. 25:1.

So by testimony of prophets, by parable, by ceremonial type, and by number, God has wrought the towering structure of fact that (1) the judgment is the harvest,—the separation of the tares from the wheat—the end of the world; that (2) the judgment, the harvest, embraces two phases, two periods: the former for the dead, the latter for the living; that (3) the one takes place according to the records in the books in the heavenly sanctuary, whereas the other takes place simultaneously in the church on earth and in the books in heaven; and that (4) the very fact that the subject is now being revealed in its fullness testifies that we are just on the verge of passing out of the former and into the latter phase and period, and that we are therefore living in the last days of earth's history.

This fourfold view of the judgment, the harvest, thus exalts the truth of it as a pearl of great price, and reveals that the depths of God's Word are unfathomable; Its wisdom inscrutable and infinite—without beginning and without end; Its fund of knowledge a perpetual fountain of truth; Its presence ever abiding; and Its beauty ineffable!

Now that the reader may be strengthened to hold fast to this fundamental and all-important truth, as well as to all other truths, we urge him to follow God's method (Inspiration) in studying the Scriptures, that he may thereby

Avoid the Many Snares.

Perhaps foremost among the multitudes who are snared while doing all they can to run away from inspired interpretation of the Scriptures are the extremists, of whom there are at least two classes: one with the tendency to literalize; the other with the tendency to spiritualize. These two will go just as far in their opposite directions, in their understanding and explaining the Scriptures, as their opposite temperaments impel them.

Take for example the Revelator's statement: ". . . I saw under the altar the souls of them that were slain for the Word of God, . . . and they cried with a loud voice, saying, How long, O Lord, holy and true, dost Thou not judge and avenge our blood?" Rev. 6:9, 10.

The literalist on the one hand, would interpret this scripture to mean that the souls were conscious and actually crying out, though the Bible is very explicit that "the dead know not anything." Eccles. 9:5. And, too, were the souls under the altar literally crying out for vengeance on their murderers, then, to be consistent, the Lord's statement, "the voice of thy brother's blood crieth unto Me from the ground" (Gen. 4:10), also the statement, "all the trees of the field shall clap their hands" (Isa. 55:12), likewise must be interpreted literally in spite of the fact that it is impossible physically for blood to cry out and for trees to clap hands.

If all, however, are obliged to admit that Abel's blood could not literally cry out, and that trees can only figuratively clap hands, then, again to be consistent, the person given to extreme literalizing should easily take hold of the actuality that "the dead know not anything," and that they are "asleep"—unconscious. He ought easily, too, to perceive that the souls of the martyrs crying for vengeance on their murderers, and that the blood of Abel crying for vengeance on his murderer, are cases virtually identical in circumstance and condition. Both of these find pointed illustration in the poetic utterance: "I hear a voice crying out, the voice of the withering field: O, Lord, pity Thou me. Let showers fall from heaven. Quench Thou my burning soul."

For one's soul to be imprisoned consciously under something for hundreds of years, with nothing to do but groaningly to languish in waiting for the resurrection morning, the while crying out for vengeance on them that spilled one's blood,—what an inexpressibly unbearable state for one's soul to be in!

The doctrine, though, of the unconscious state of the dead not only puts at peace the worried human mind but also ascribes to God mercy and love toward helpless human beings, thus being the only position on the subject that can lead the sinner rationally to love God and to trust in Him.

To the one who on the other hand is inclined oppositely, to spiritualize the souls, the slaughter, the heavens, the new earth, etc.,—to him these have neither individuality nor reality. And when concerning the doctrine of the slaughter he is asked the simple question, What kind of slaughter would a spiritual one be? he is at a loss to answer!

For all, there exists in this connection one great need: the Spirit of Truth, Whose right alone it is to interpret the Scriptures.

The most common cause of doctrinal confusion among Bible students lies in their so very frequently failing to view a subject in full perspective from the writer's point of view,—a failing which results in their seeing it from some foreign standpoint so narrowing their view that instead of gaining the writer's idea on the subject, they gain a false idea on it. And if the idea be to their liking, they magnify and zealously promote it as truth, whereas if it be not to their liking, they vigorously oppose it, and then lay it to the responsibility of the writer!

To illustrate thus getting a wrong idea of a thing from a wrong view of it: a child who accompanies his mother to a zoo, and who has never seen a peacock, suddenly comes upon one in full tail-spread going away from him, and creating to his uninitiated eyes the illusion of a large walking fan!

Thrilled with the illusory wonder before him he excitedly exclaims the sight, only to have mother disenchant him with the disillusioning assurance that it is only a peacock! On another occasion, however, when accompanying his father to the zoo, the child again sees a peacock, but this time in full front view presenting a sight apparently entirely new and different. Quickly he turns with excited questions to his father, who tells him that it is a peacock!

Whereupon the argument begins, with the son protesting that the peacock which he and his mother had seen, looked nothing like this one. And unable to reconcile, as simply major and minor aspects of the same thing, that which he now sees from the front, or main point of view, and that which he before saw from the rear, or foreign point of view, his mind gropes in confusion wondering whether to believe Father or Mother.

So it is with the Bible when one looks at a subject from a standpoint foreign to the author's. He finds discrepancies in the position held by the one who sees the subject through the author's eyes. In order, consequently, to maintain the false idea resulting from his foreign point of view, he is led to resort to outside sources: to one commentator or the other; to this version or to that; to technicalities and inferences of language: in the Greek, in the Hebrew, in this, in that, or in the other (languages, none of which it is likely he himself either reads or writes); or to referring to this or that so-called original manuscript (which in all probability he has never seen).

At the end of this long winding road, he has succeeded only in magnifying from a mole hill to a mountain one passage of scripture, and in reducing from a mountain to a mole hill, or entirely setting aside, another passage of scripture, all because the Bible, which the Lord has placed in his hands, does not support his idea. These pretentious procedures are calculated to demonstrate his scholarly attainments in the hope of lending to his false idea such an appearance of authority as to compel their acceptance by all who come in contact with his theory.

Concretely: It is never fair when treating of the subject of the judgment, to give *first* and *foremost* consideration to any writing which deals directly with the subject of salvation, while only incidentally referring to the subject of the judgment. Take for example Paul's statement:

"Which hope we have as an anchor of the soul both sure and steadfast, and which entereth into that within the vail; whither the forerunner is for us entered, even Jesus, made an high priest for ever after the order of Melchisedec." Heb. 6:19, 20.

Instead of viewing the content of these verses in the light of all that is revealed on the subject, a procedure which would insure the verses' reflecting the author's thought, some Bible students, losing sight of Paul's point of view, magnify out of all due proportion the importance of these verses' statement, thus placing upon it constructions which, though perhaps plausible enough when taken alone are manifestly strained, warped, and untenable when viewed in the light of all other scriptures bearing on the subject. Such wresting, needless to say, is unfair to the author, perilous to the one affected, and criminal of the wrester.

To illustrate the matter still further and more extensively: Surrounding a table are six Bible students and an infidel. On one side are Peter, James, and John; on the other, Black, Brown, and Green; while at one end is the infidel. He listens attentively to the six discussing Christ's ministry after His ascension, in the light of Hebrews 6:19, 20; 9:12, 26—

"Which hope we have as an anchor of the soul, both sure and steadfast, and which entereth into that within the vail; whither the forerunner is for us entered, even Jesus, made an high priest for ever after the order of Melchisedec." Heb. 6:19, 20.

"Neither by the blood of goats and calves, but by His Own blood He entered in once into the holy place, having obtained eternal redemption for us." Heb. 9:12.

"For then must He often have suffered since the foundation of the world: but now once in the end of the world hath He appeared to put away sin by the sacrifice of Himself." Heb. 9:26.

Peter, James, and John, sharing the author's perspective, are in full agreement that one cannot, on a scripture treating of salvation, and only incidentally referring to Christ's ministry, build up a correct basic understanding of that ministry, but rather that one must take the writings of the prophets which deal directly with the sanctuary and its service, and then harmonize Paul's writings with the prophets', not the prophets' with Paul's.

So far as Peter, James, and John are concerned, the discussion results in their arriving at the conclusion that Paul, in order to be in agreement with both himself and the prophets, must be understood in Hebrews 6:19 to be speaking in prophetic past (that is, future in fact, though present or past in tense), and that therefore he is pointing to the time that his converts are, with Christ, "once in the end of the world" (Heb. 9:26), to enter "within the vail," "whither the forerunner [Christ] is for us entered." Heb. 6:20. When?—not in Paul's time but now, "in the end of the world," His having first "entered in once into the holy place." Heb. 9:12.

Black, Brown, and Green, however, from their foreign points of view on these verses, are in disagreement even among themselves: Black, stressing Hebrews 6:19, 20, is convinced that Paul teaches that Christ entered the Most Holy apartment immediately after His ascension; Brown, holding to Hebrews 9:12, is positive that Christ entered, not the Most Holy, but the holy apartment; and Green, on the weight of verse 26, insists that Christ is to enter the sanctuary "once in the end of the world," after His second coming.

Still seeing from their foreign points of view, Black further argues that by the term, "the holy," Paul means the "Holiest of all," while Brown counters that if Paul loosely uses the term "holy" for the "Holiest of all," then how can one possibly know that when he says the "Holiest of all," he does not mean the "holy"?

Then on the strength of Moses' statement, "Speak unto Aaron thy brother, that he come not at all times into the holy place within the vail before the mercy seat, which is upon the ark" (Lev. 16:2), Black furthermore holds that Paul, in the words, "But by His own blood He entered . . . into the holy place" (Heb. 9:12), refers to "the Holiest of all" Heb. 9:3. But Peter insists that to construe Paul's use of the term "holy place" to mean the "Holiest of all," is both unreasonable and unfair, for no writer in clear mind, speaking of both apartments, will indiscriminately interchange the terms, and yet expect his readers accurately to comprehend the idea he is putting forth. Black, however, retorts that Moses uses the term "holy place" (Lev. 16:2) when speaking of the second apartment.

In reply to this, Peter protests that Moses does so because whereas he calls the second apartment "the holy place within the vail," he calls the first apartment "the tabernacle of the congregation" (verse 16), while Paul chooses to term the first apartment "the holy place," and the second apartment, "the Holiest of all."

Again: Peter insists that if, in Paul's writings, where both apartments are discussed, one is justified in interpreting "the holy" to mean "Holiest of all," then another, by the same token of logic, is equally justified in interpreting the "Holiest of all" to mean the "holy."

Though Peter's clear-cut logic completely dissipates the force of Black's contention, yet, because of the wide differences of opinion among a group of Christian believers, the final result of the discussion is that what the harmony among Peter, John, and James did toward converting the infidel to Christianity, Black's, Brown's, and Green's disagreeing with one another, also Black's disagreeing with Peter, counteracted. This discord confirmed the infidel in his infidelity, leaving him fully persuaded that Christianity is but a stupendous bubble; whereupon Satan, in diabolic glee, gives to Black, Brown, and Green, "his seat, and great authority." And Christendom, already rife with doctrinal confusion, continues to bristle with schismatic strife, nurturing infidels in their hostility to Christianity, instead of converting them to it!

If Christ pronounces a woe upon those who refuse to give a glass of cold water to the least of His followers, what will be the condemnation and end of such as Black, Brown, and Green, who, by their spirit of self-aggrandizement, scatter from Christ while professing to gather with Him!

Never is it right to interpret any scripture isolated from its context, for to do so is automatically to do violence to its meaning.

For instance, the scripture, "But, beloved, be not ignorant of this one thing, that one day is with the Lord as a thousand years, and a thousand years as one day" (2 Pet. 3:8), taken by itself, has suffered various interpretations, only adding to the confusion and doubts already permeating the Christian world. But only one interpretation will it admit when taken with its context: "Knowing this first, that there shall come in the last days scoffers, walking after their own lusts, and saying, Where is the promise of His coming? for since the fathers fell asleep, all things continue as they were from the beginning of the creation." Verses 3, 4.

From this contextual setting, we see that in the verse in point the apostle is endeavoring by figurative language to show that the scoffers whom he saw would arise in our day, though attempting to overthrow the faith of those believing in Moses' account of the flood and awaiting the Lord's returning, are unwittingly but scoffing at their own blindness. For they cannot see that that which seems to them, by the gauge of their short-lived days, an ever-present delay in the Lord's second coming, is to the Eternal One but a fleeting moment of waiting, and that their finite wisdom is consequently but foolishness. And, contrariwise, what they regard as time too short and worthless for practical use, the Lord regards as very long and very precious in our short lives.

Clearly, therefore, when this scripture is interpreted according to its context, human measurements of time are seen not to be God's measurements, just as human thoughts are not His thoughts (Isa. 55:7, 8).

The light of this example makes clear that just as a safety valve is necessary to keep a boiler from exploding with excess pressure, so only a faithful regard to the context of a scripture can keep its interpreter from exploding with theories and ideas foreign to the Scriptures.

When those who love the truth study any doctrinal subject, they never, in trying to harmonize their private opinions with a scripture in point, leave the scripture so interpreted as to contradict either other portions of the Bible or the position of constituted authority, but rather they forsake their opinions.

Having taken a wrong view on the subject of the judgment, some have, though unknowingly, tried in reality to change its correct time and true nature, rather than to maintain them. This unwitting endeavor has in turn led them to take wrong views on many other Bible truths. The fact, though, that this great hub-doctrine still remains intact and solid, is unimpeachable evidence that likewise do all its spoke-doctrines.

Those who have undertaken to interpret the Scriptures independently of Inspiration, a private exercise which is contrary to the injunction given in 2 Peter 1:20, 21, and those who have accepted such views, will, unless they now forsake their errors for the truth, one day find themselves the victims of the disastrous circumstances with which they have bound themselves, and will be terribly confounded as they hear the horrifying pronouncement: "I have not spoken to them, yet they prophesied"; "depart from Me, ye that work iniquity." Jer. 23:21; Matt. 7:23.

May they, therefore, while probation still lingers and the blood of Christ is yet available to atone for the sins of all, "give the more earnest heed" to the solemn declaration of

The First Angel's Message.

"Fear God, and give glory to Him; for the hour of his judgment is come." Rev. 14:7.

To clear the appointed time of this message, we must take into consideration that from the fourth to the twenty-second chapter of The Revelation, its theme is continuous. This is seen from the conjunction "and," which, beginning each chapter, shows that all these revelations were given to John at the time that the "Voice" said to him: "Come up hither, and I will shew thee things which must be hereafter" (Rev. 4:1)—things which were to come to pass sometime after he had the vision of them. And John having had this vision about 96

A. D., the first angel's message therefore could not possibly have been preached be-fore that time, as some think it was; for, to repeat, he was not shown the things of the past, but the things of the future.

Again: the fact that he says, "I saw another [the first] angel . . . having the everlasting gospel to preach," further shows that this angel's message had not been preached before he had the vision, but that it was to be preached in the future from that time.

There is not, moreover, either scripture or church history to show that the judgment began in or before John's time. And still further, as the first angel's mes-sage was never preached before 1844, then when the judgment hour came, this angel's message—the mes-sage concerning the judgment—went forth.

The investigative judgment being in two sections (the first, devoted to the dead; the second, to the liv-ing), the fact is evidenced that though the first, the second, and the third angels' messages (Rev. 14:6-12) apply directly to the period of the judgment of the living, they must also, though indirectly, apply to the period of the judgment of the dead. In this relation only, except as a warning of coming events, have they been preached since 1844. When, therefore, the judg-ment of the living commences and the image of the beast is fully made up, then these messages are, with a loud cry, to be repeated as present truth concerning the living instead of the dead.

Thus drawn into sharp focus, the facts concerning the eternal (the administrative) throne, the provisional (the mediatorial-judicial) throne, and the judgment, conclusively vindicate the position established by the book which was used in the proclamation of the first, second, and third angels' messages in their first application, and which in the voice of its writer, declares:

"I saw the Father rise from the throne, and in a flaming chariot go into the holy of holies within the vail, and sit down. Then Jesus rose up from the throne, and the most of those who were bowed down arose with Him. I did not see one ray of light pass from Jesus to the careless multitude after He arose, and they were left in perfect darkness. Those who arose when Jesus did, kept their eyes fixed on Him as He left the throne and led them out a little way. Then He raised His right arm, and we heard His lovely voice saying, 'Wait here; I am going to My Father to receive the kingdom; keep your garments spotless, and in a little while I will return from the wedding and receive you to Myself.' Then a cloudy chariot, with wheels like flaming fire, surrounded by angels, came to where Jesus was. He stepped into the chariot and was borne to the holiest, where the Father sat. There I beheld Jesus, a great High

Priest, standing before the Father."—*Early Writings*, p. 55.

This transfer from the administrative throne to the mediatorial-judicial throne, being made to investigate those wedding guests who are now dead, leads to the following

Questions and Answers.

1. *Did Christ Preach to the Dead?*

1 Pet. 3:18-20.

"For Christ also," answers Peter in the same scripture giving rise to this question, "hath once suffered for sins, the just for the unjust, that He might bring us to God, being put to death in the flesh, but quickened by the spirit: by which also He went and preached unto the spirits in prison; which sometime were disobedient, when once the longsuffering of God waited in the days of Noah, while the ark was a preparing, wherein few, that is, eight souls were saved by water." 1 Pet. 3:18-20.

Obviously enough, Peter is not here saying that Christ, while His body lay in the tomb, preached to the spirits in prison, as is understood by some; but rather simply that through the medium of the Spirit by Whom He was resurrected, He preached to them "in the days of Noah, while the ark was a preparing." Nor does it say that Christ preached to the dead, but rather "unto the spirits in prison." The concern, therefore, as to whether "the spirits in prison" mean the dead or the living, is a matter of interpretation, and such an interpretation must come of divine authority.

When speaking of the dead, the Bible never calls them spirits. It does, however, so designate the living. It plainly says, moreover, that "the dead know not anything, neither have they any more a reward; for the memory of them is forgotten. Also their love, and their hatred, and their envy, is now perished; neither have they any more a portion for ever in any thing that is done under the sun." Eccles. 9:5, 6.

Still further, in the parable of the rich man and Lazarus, the Lord makes exceedingly plain that after death the sinner has no chance at all for salvation; no, not even for a drop of cold water on his tongue, as is memorably witnessed by the rich man's being denied his plea in death: "Son, remember that thou in thy lifetime receivedst thy good things, and likewise Lazarus evil things: but now he is comforted, and thou art tormented. And beside all this, between us and you there is a great gulf fixed: so that they which would pass from hence to you cannot; neither can they pass to us, that would come from thence." Luke 16:25, 26.

Here, unforgettably, we are shown that the only way any of us can be saved from hell's torment is to "hear . . . Moses and the prophets" while we are yet alive, and that if we hear them not, then the Lord cannot help us after death; also that if we are not persuaded by them, neither will we "be persuaded, though one rose from the dead." Luke 16:29-31. There consequently not being any chance for salvation after death, then if any, while living, have failed to hear "Moses and the prophets," why should Christ preach to them after they have died? "God is not the God of the dead, but of the living." Matt. 22:32.

The "spirits in prison" cannot, accordingly, be any others than the antediluvians, to whom Christ, in the person of His Spirit, Who raised Him, preached aforetime through Noah, and to whom the Spirit's warning was of no moment, with the fearful result that by their refusal to hear His pleadings, they became figuratively imprisoned by the circumstances of the coming flood, from the certain consequences of which they could not escape.

The statement, moreover, "wherein few, that is, eight souls were saved by water," further shows that it was by His Spirit in Noah's preaching that Christ before the flood visited the spirits in prison and saved eight souls—Noah and his family. Thus "the Spirit of Christ which was in" "the prophets," also "did signify, when It testified beforehand the sufferings of Christ, and the glory that should follow." 1 Pet. 1:10, 11.

But if it is true, asks someone, that Christ did not preach to the dead, then what about those dead who were

2. *Left Without a Chance?*

The law of death cannot be reversed by Anyone's ignorance of God. And, furthermore, "When I say unto the wicked," says the Lord to His prophet, "Thou shalt surely die; and thou givest him not warning, nor speakest to warn the wicked from his wicked way, to save his life; the same wicked man shall die in his iniquity; but his blood will I require at thine hand." Ezek. 3:18.

This scripture clearly teaches that those who have died in their sins, because of the neglect of the watchman, cannot be rescued, and that their blood shall be required at the hand of the watchman responsible for their fate of being unsaved and left without a chance.

To be consistent, then, those who have died in their sins through their own neglect, either ignorantly or willfully, as did the antediluvian world, rather than through neglect of the watchmen, would be even less excusable than the former class, and would have even less right than they (who have no right at all) to be preached to after death, even were it possible.

And those who have never had a chance to hear the prophets, to them "the heavens declare the glory of God; and the firmament sheweth His handiwork. Day unto day uttereth speech, and night unto night sheweth knowledge. There is no speech nor language, where their voice is not heard." Ps. 19:1-3.

All mankind are therefore to be judged according to the measure of light which God has turned upon their way, and according to their desire to walk in the light. And those who unfortunately have failed to learn of Him and to know the exact truth, will not be condemned for having believed an error while they were in the darkness, but "this is the condemnation," says the Lord, "that light is come into the world, and men loved darkness rather than light, because their deeds were evil." John 3:19.

In the full light of the combined facts on the subject, very obvious is the certainty that the Scriptures do not certify a doc-trine of a second chance. But in an effort to prove that they do, those who advocate the doctrine challengingly bring the apostle's question: "What shall they do which are

3. *"Baptized for the Dead?"*

1 Cor. 15:29.

Speaking to the Corinthians, the apostle Paul makes plain that if there is no resurrection of the dead, then neither is there salvation in Christ:

"And if Christ be not risen, then is our preaching vain, and your faith is also vain. Yea, and we are found false witnesses of God; because we have testified of God that He raised up Christ: Whom He raised not up, if so be that the dead rise not. For if the dead rise not, then is not Christ raised: and if Christ be not raised, your faith is vain; ye are yet in your sins. Then they also which are fallen asleep in Christ are perished. If in this life only we have hope in Christ, we are of all men most miserable. But now is Christ risen from the dead, and become the first fruits of them that slept. For since by man came death, by man came also the resurrection of the dead. For as in Adam all die, even so in Christ shall all be made alive. But every man in his own order: Christ the first fruits; afterward they that are Christ's at His coming. . . . Else what shall they do which are baptized for the dead, if the dead rise not at all? Why are they then baptized for the dead?" 1 Cor. 15:14-22, 29.

This scripture does not teach that the living must be baptized for the dead: for Paul is not calling into question the effect that the baptism would have on the dead, but rather the effect it would have on the living: "What," he asks, "shall they [the living] do which are baptized for the dead?" Not: what shall the dead do, for whom we, the living, have been baptized.

Consequently, the statement, "baptized

for the dead," teaches that baptism for the dead is for the benefit of those only who are themselves baptized while living. In other words, they are baptized, not in the hope of living until the Lord comes to take them to the everlasting mansions above, but in the hope of rising from the dead on the resurrection day. Hence the question: "if the dead rise not at all . . . why are they then baptized?"

From this elucidation of the subject, the saints who are baptized for the dead are clearly seen to be those who pass through the state of death. And, inferentially, those who shall be baptized about the time of Christ's coming, to make up that immortal company of living saints who shall be awaiting His triumphal return, with all His angels, are seen, equally as clearly, to be baptized for the living—never to pass through the state of death!

And finally, if the early Christians were to baptize themselves for others who had died without baptism, such a commandment would have been given in the Scriptures, and such baptismal services would have been recorded: the Bible, though, commands baptism only for the living, to whom it says: "Repent, and be baptized." Acts 2:38.

That the sincere Bible student might know the saving truth for this time; that knowing it, he might follow it whithersoever it leads; that if he be baptized for the dead, he might be among the resurrected just, or if he be baptized for the living, he might be among the translated: in either case being changed "in a moment, in the twinkling of an eye" (1 Cor. 15:52), forever to be among the redeemed immortals, delivered from pain and sorrow, having entered into life and joy everlasting,—this, dear reader, is the sole object in publishing and getting into your hands this truth-laden booklet. If you are determined to enter into the glory it reveals, you will gratefully heed *its* clear-ringing lesson to

Let Your Faith Now Be Practical, Not Theoretical Only.

As a religion that leaves the dead without resurrection and the living without translation is as good as nothing, just so is the doctrine of the Bible when divorced from practice. Though "theoretical discourses are essential, that all may know the form of doctrine, and see the chain of truth, link after link, uniting in a perfect whole. . . . no discourse should ever be delivered without presenting Christ and Him crucified as the foundation of the gospel, making a practical application of the truths set forth, and impressing upon the people the fact that the doctrine of Christ is not yea and nay, but yea and amen in Christ Jesus."—*Testimonies*, Vol. 4, pp. 394, 395.

"Satan offers to men the kingdoms of the world if they will yield to him the supremacy. Many do this, and sacrifice

Heaven. It is better to die than to sin; better to want than to defraud; better to hunger than to lie. Let all who are tempted, meet Satan with these words: 'Blessed is everyone that feareth the Lord, that walketh in His ways. For thou shalt meet the labor of thine hands; happy shalt thou be, and it shall be well with thee.' Here is a condition and a promise which will be unmistakably realized. Happiness and prosperity will be the result of serving the Lord."—*Id.*, p. 495.

"Therefore leaving the principles of the doctrine of Christ, let us go on unto perfection; not laying again the foundation of repentance from dead works, and of faith toward God" (Heb. 6:1), or forgetting that "all scripture is given by Inspiration of God, and is profitable for doctrine, for reproof, for correction, for instruction in righteousness: that the man of God may be perfect, thoroughly furnished unto all good works." 2 Tim. 3:16, 17.

(All Italics ours)

TOPICAL INDEX

TOPICAL INDEX—(Cont.)

SCRIPTURAL INDEX

SCRIPTURAL INDEX—(Cont.)

SCRIPTURAL INDEX—(Cont.)